To Myelle,

No Ordinary Cats

By Lisa Erixon

Lisa Erixon

One Printers Way
Altona, MB R0G 0B0
Canada

www.friesenpress.com

ISBN
978-1-03-916089-7 (Hardcover)
978-1-03-916088-0 (Paperback)
978-1-03-916090-3 (eBook)

1. Pets, Cats

Distributed to the trade by The Ingram Book Company

"Those who teach us the most about humanity aren't always human."

– Donald L Hicks

· ·

This story is dedicated in loving memory of those cats whose presence made my life infinitely richer:

Maxx

Riser and Dilly

Angel

Moonsie and Bandit

Chuck

Chairman Meow and Fluffity

And to those cats whose affection I appreciate daily:

Misty and Smokey

*permission to use granted by author Donald L. Hicks

I glance over at the three tiny balls of fur snuggled together in the carrier. The movement of the car is making them drowsy. Their little eyes keep closing; apparently, my singing of classic rock numbers isn't very entertaining either.

The arrival of new kittens always causes me to be introspective. Their presence is a reminder of all of the cats that have owned me. And I am under no illusions – they have indeed owned me. But each of them has taught me valuable lessons. It could be something as simple as "take time for a nap" or something more practical, like the importance of good grooming. Regardless of the lessons taught, their presence in my life has brought me great joy – their deaths, immense sorrow.

If I had my druthers, I would have indoor cats, outdoor cats, and in-between cats. If I didn't have someone around to rein me in, I would probably be one of those stereotypical crazy cat ladies, skimping on her groceries in order to feed her charges. Cats were a constant in my childhood, and I loved their widely varying personalities. My love for the species has been passed down to my sons, based on their constant childhood interactions with them.

We are almost home. The deceleration of the car wakes the kittens. They stand up on shaky legs and jostle around the interior of the carrier like tiny bumper cars. I bring the car to a stop and take the carrier into my garage. I lift the latch on the door and open it wide, taking care to make sure it won't swing back and startle them. Now that they are here, they are in no hurry to leave the carrier's comparative safety and security.

I lift the first kitten from the carrier. A tiny female with faint calico markings, she doesn't protest as I set her on my knee for a closer examination. She has the most gorgeous eyes and her whiskers are almost longer than she is. The second kitten, a larger male, makes a bit of a fuss when he is removed from the carrier. I smile at his spunk and set him down beside his sister. His fur is a sleek and shiny black, and he sports white whiskers and tiny white claws. The last kitten takes a little more convincing to get out of the carrier and seems to want to cuddle. I have no objection. His longer hair is tawny and silky with lovely dark dapples.

Part of the joy of having new kittens is the naming process. Some names come very easily, but others take time and aren't administered until a distinct or unique facet of that cat's personality or appearance has manifested. Proper names are only really useful on the rare occasion when a cat is taken to the vet — most of our cats end up with nicknames, some beyond ludicrous. My grandmother had a cat, given the time-honoured name of Tom, who spent most of his time on her verandah when he should have been hanging out in the barn with his cohorts. No matter the season or weather, his presence on the verandah was a given. He didn't even seem to mind the extreme cold and was eventually rechristened "NumNutz."

The last kitten wants down to join his littermates. I watch as they begin their first tentative exploration of the space that will be their home. There are corners of the garage to be examined, summer cushions to be sniffed, and some scraps of yesterday's roast beef to taste.

Welcome, little ones. I've been waiting for you.

No
Ordinary
Cats

CHAPTER ONE

· · · · · · · · · · · · · · · · · ·

MAXX

*Y*ou have got *to be kidding me,* Maxx thought. *You're stuffing me into that lousy carrier* again?

Her strenuous protests made no difference. The older human, in whose house she'd been living for the last two years, shoved her rudely into the cracked and dusty carrier.

Well, Maxx thought, *here we go again…*

The carrier was placed in the older human's car, and the door slammed. During the lengthy trip to what Maxx assumed would be her next new home, she had time to reflect on the other places in which she'd lived.

She was born in a ramshackle barn held together primarily by spider webs. One of a litter of four, she and her only other surviving littermate were removed from the barn and taken to live in a home nearby. She was given the name Maxx, and her littermate was named P.B., short for "Poor Baby." P.B. had problems with her eyes as a young kitten, which led to vision problems for the rest of her short life.

In the new home, life was quite tolerable. Maxx was that enviable creature known as an indoor-outdoor cat – freedom to roam at will, yet having a comfortable indoor place to sleep and an absolutely perfect old sofa downstairs on which to sharpen her claws. Three humans, a mother and two daughters, lived in the home as well; all of them treated her with respect and affection.

When one of the daughters moved to a new town, she took Maxx with her for company. It was a very short-lived arrangement. Maxx was unhappy with all of it. The furniture was all in the wrong spots, her litter box smelled odd, she was scolded for sharpening her claws on the sofa, and outside, the stunted trees stank of dog. After yowling for three straight nights, coughing up hairballs, and doing her business in a large potted plant, she was unceremoniously returned home.

A few years later, she moved to a new home with the older human, who decided to take up residence in a city. But city life did not suit Maxx either. She expressed her dissatisfaction with *that* living situation in a multitude of ways: doing her business in the flowerbeds, running away for days at a time and shredding the living room drapes.

The older human eventually lost patience with Maxx's impatience – hence, the latest deportation to yet another home.

In the carrier, Maxx sighed deeply. She was an old cat, with an old cat's distinct aversion to change. The car finally slowed and drew to a stop. The older human removed the carrier and set it on the grass with a sigh of relief.

Maxx looked around her with little interest. Yes, there were lots of trees, but what use was a tree to an old cat who didn't climb them any longer? And yes, she could hear birds, but what was the point when she couldn't catch them any longer either? Ah, birds. She had loved to catch birds as a young cat; she could snatch a swallow out of mid-air as it dive-bombed her on the grass.

The carrier door opened, and Maxx stepped out cautiously. She could see an old shed nearby. *That's where I'll likely have to sleep,* she thought morosely.

An old barn was situated across the road. *That's probably where I'll have to find my own dinner,* she thought more morosely still.

A tiny human came barrelling toward her. *I might have to forget I don't climb trees,* Maxx thought in panic.

But the tiny human stopped in front of her and dropped to its knees. A small, grimy hand reached out and gently patted her back. Behind the tiny human was a human she knew. It was the human in whose house she had spent four memorable days, years ago.

Well, Maxx thought, *I'm not sure how* this *is going to work out. And I don't think I'm going to have any use for a tiny human. What can it do to make my life easier?*

But she was wrong. She did have a use for the tiny human, who was a little boy, and for his younger brother who followed. They gave her love. Complete and unconditional love such as she had never experienced before. And she found to her absolute astonishment that she adored them. She may have been an old cat with a crusty heart and achy joints, but she forgot all of that when she was in the company of the tiny humans.

There was only one problem. And its name was Bruce, nicknamed Brewster. He was a large, senseless, black and white spotted dog with a penchant for chasing anything that moved – and many things that didn't, like his own tail. On Maxx's first day in her new home, she and Bruce had a slight altercation. He chased her weary old bones a few feet up a nearby maple tree, and Maxx was extremely unhappy. She made her stiff and awkward way down, and decided that they needed to come to an immediate understanding.

"Look, Dog, I know you were here first and that gives you some rights. However, I'm here now too. And we have to get some things straight."

"Like what?" Bruce gazed at her blankly, his tongue lolling to one side. Maxx rolled her eyes and tried again.

"Let me clarify it for you. You don't chase me, and I won't have to scratch your eyes out. Did you get that? You: No chase. Me: No run."

He ignored her, flopped down, and engaged in a very thorough licking of his private dog bits. Maxx shook her head. She had never lived in close proximity to a dog before and was unsure if she was going to be able to train him.

However, as the weeks passed, she and Bruce reached a truce. It only took four different occasions of swiping her claws across his nose, but Bruce finally understood that he wasn't supposed to chase Maxx.

Without Maxx to chase, Bruce resorted to his previous forms of entertainment: chasing traffic through the yard, chasing traffic out of the yard, and chasing traffic up the road. The possibilities were endless. After one such occasion, Maxx shook her head as Bruce, tongue lolling and panting in exhaustion, dragged his tired carcass back to the house.

"Why on earth do you do that? You know you're never going to catch them. And if you ever slipped, you could really get hurt." Maxx surprised even herself with her concern for Bruce.

"Yeah, but I have to keep the trucks away from the little humans. That's my job!" he exclaimed between noisy slurps in the water dish. "Gotta keep 'em safe. That's what I do."

He made his way under the deck into one of the many holes he had dug to keep cool in the summer heat. Maxx watched him turn around three times. She didn't understand why he did that – did he think the hole was going to suddenly change in size on the third rotation?

Dogs, she thought. *Strange creatures.*

One lazy summer afternoon, a strange car drove into the yard and stopped. All of her humans were away, but Maxx watched the car without concern from her spot under a deck chair. However, as its occupant climbed out, she sat up straighter, eyes narrowing, and hissed at Bruce, who was lounging under the deck.

"Hey, Bruce! *Bruce! Wake up!*"

Bruce sleepily lifted his head. "What's the problem?"

"See that human? *That's* the one who likes stuffing me in the carrier. *That's* the one who swatted me when I did my business in her flower-bed. *That's* the one who wouldn't let me climb her new curtains!"

Bruce looked at the intruder with more interest. "What do you want me to do?"

"Chase her, Bruce! Get her! *Jump up on her!*" Max yowled.

"This is gonna be fun!" Bruce lumbered out from under the deck, and he galloped toward Maxx's grumpy human, who was holding a large, flat box in both hands. Making good on his promise, he jumped up, knocking the container to the ground. Cursing Bruce and all dogs before and after him, the grumpy human tried to get away, but Bruce continued to leap around her, jumping up occasionally for a sloppy kiss, one of which knocked her glasses askew.

When the human and the tiny humans drove into the yard a little later, they found Bruce looking up adoringly at his very grumpy quarry, who was standing on top of the picnic table, holding a stout branch in one hand. Maxx was licking at the sticky, melting mess on the ground: the remnants of an ice-cream birthday cake.

Later that night, Maxx padded over to the tree to which Bruce had been tied. His head rested on his front paws; he looked up at her sadly. "They only tie me up when I've done something wrong. Did I do a bad thing?"

"Nope," Maxx told him affectionately. "You did exactly right. You're a good dog. Goofy, but good." Bruce gave her a swipe with his tongue that nearly knocked her off her feet. Maxx chuckled again as she recalled the afternoon's events and Bruce's part in them. "You're a good dog, Brucie. Thank you."

As the tiny humans grew, they included Maxx in their indoor and outdoor games. The tiny humans cuddled her, lugged her around in less-than-dignified ways, and fed her delicious snacks. They made sure she had lots of food and water, and helped build her winter home. She was warm, comfortable, and loved.

Their excellent care and attention, however, could not mitigate the ravages of the advancing years. Walking was painful, her fur was losing its shine because she was no longer capable of grooming it efficiently, and both her sight and hearing were failing rapidly.

There's one thing an old cat knows — and she knows it as well as the name she is given or the humans she can trust — she knows when it is her time. Cats don't like to make a fuss when they're sick or when they sense they're nearing the end of their lives. If they have any control over the situation and the mobility of their legs, they will leave quietly and without fanfare. And they don't come back.

Maxx knew it was time to go. She would miss her humans. And she would miss Bruce.

What will he do without me? she thought with a pang of regret.

He was also old — too old to adjust to someone new. Her resolution briefly wavered, but the compulsion to go outweighed the longing to stay. As she climbed stiffly down from the deck, she hoped the humans wouldn't mourn her for long.

I hope there will soon be new cats here for the humans to love, she thought with gratitude. *Like they loved me.*

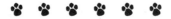

Though she and I hadn't always been the best of friends, I found I missed Maxx tremendously. So did my boys. I appreciated that she had always been gentle with them when they were very young. Her long life taught me that you should always be open to the possibility of love, regardless of its source.

Due to his advancing age, it became necessary to euthanize Bruce shortly after Maxx's passing. We'd had two gentle animal souls – now, we had none.

A few months later, a work colleague revealed that he had two house cats to rehome. My hand was the first in the air to take them. And so Terrence and Phyllis came into our lives.

CHAPTER TWO

· ·

TERRENCE
AND PHYLLIS

An explosive sneeze erupted from the human with long dark hair. She wiped her nose continually and rubbed at her eyes. She looked at the two cats lounging on the sofa nearby with barely disguised resentment. She sighed and wiped her nose once more.

The cats had grown used to her noises, and they barely registered anymore. The cats were tucked in so close to each other that it was hard to tell where one cat ended and the other began. They were a matched pair of tabbies with amber eyes, dark stripes, and white chins.

With unerring feline instinct, Terrence had begun to sense they were wearing out their welcome. It wasn't as if the other human who lived in the house resented them. On the contrary, he showered them with compliments, brushed them regularly, kept their food and water dishes full, and didn't complain, even when Terrence sharpened his claws on the back of the sofa. And Terrence liked to keep his claws sharp.

Another sneeze exploded from the dark-haired human; she bounced up from the sofa in disgust and disappeared.

Phyllis lifted her head and yawned. "About time. I was getting tired of listening to her wheezes and snorts."

Terrence sat up and looked in the direction the human had gone. "I don't like listening to her, either, but I think there's something about us that really bothers her. She makes those noises all the time and I don't think humans are supposed to do that. I think there's a good possibility we might have to leave."

"Leave?" Phyllis was alarmed. "Where would we go? And why would *we* have to leave? Can't *she* leave? We've been here longer than she has!"

"I don't think that's going to matter," Terrence replied sharply. "You'd better start getting used to the idea."

Phyllis leaped nimbly to the top of the sofa and then disappeared from sight behind it. A second later, Terrence heard her claws viciously ripping away at the fabric on its back.

Yup, Terrence thought, *there she is, getting used to the idea of leaving.*

Terrence's premonition proved correct. A few days later, he and Phyllis were bundled into a cat carrier. The noisy human with the long hair looked triumphant, while the other human was devastated. He bent down over the carrier, looked into Terrence and Phyllis's faces, and then turned away sadly.

The carrier was placed in the back seat of a different car than the one they knew. Two small humans sat on either side of them. The cats could tell that the small humans were excited to see them. They talked to them in high-pitched voices and stuck their thin fingers through the carrier in an attempt to stroke their fur.

Phyllis shrank away from both the chatter and the fingers. She had no experience with small humans and had no idea what to do with them. Terrence, however, looked at them with interest. He had always felt, in his secret feline soul, that there were more and differing types

9

of humans out there than the two they'd been exposed to. And he was eager to find out if that was true.

The ride to their new home was brief, and their carrier was gently set down inside an open garage. When the carrier door was opened, eager hands reached in. Terrence was lifted into skinny arms and immediately cuddled. He liked the smell and caresses of this small human and snuggled closer.

Phyllis sank her claws into the rough towel lining the bottom of the carrier and hung on as the second small human tugged her out. She and the towel ended up on the dusty garage floor. The small human didn't pick her up but flopped down on his stomach beside her and looked directly into her eyes. He spoke to her softly and with a gentle hand, stroked her back. Phyllis arched up into the caress, and the bond was sealed.

It's a curious thing. House cats look down on outdoor cats because they are wild and uncivilized. Why would you want to go hunting for food when a human will bring it to you? Why scratch in the dirt or the snow to do your business when a human will not only give you a place to do it but clean it up afterward? Why would you want to get your fur dusty and your tail full of sticky things that are painful to remove?

Outdoor cats look down on their indoor brethren. A pampered life is for sissies. Get out here and earn your keep. Feel the wind in your whiskers and learn for yourself the charm of falling asleep with the sound of the rustling poplar leaves as a lullaby.

Terrence, renamed Terrorizer (which he secretly adored) or Riser for short, and Phyllis (renamed Dilly) thought they might find it difficult to get used to outdoor life. They had rarely been outdoors in their former home, only leaving it briefly to be carried to a car. But to their amazement, they took to outdoor life almost immediately. The space! The ability to go wherever they wanted! And the small grey things that scurried everywhere and were ridiculously tasty! And look at those red, furry, scolding, chattering things in the trees! They loved it all.

On their travels around their new home, they discovered other cats. These cats were distrustful and wary, and bolted as soon as they were seen.

Dilly, especially, wondered about them. Why didn't the human who belonged to her and Riser belong to them too? Didn't they want to know what it was like to be cared for and loved? It was a puzzle.

Their small humans made sure they had indoor time too. Soft cushions, warm milk, tasty treats, and lots of attention were all theirs for the taking. Being here far outweighed their former home, where they were alone much of the time.

The only downside to indoor time came when they were sometimes rapidly ejected outside. Riser and Dilly might be comfortably snoozing when they were scooped up by small human hands and carried quickly to the sliding door. There would be a pause there, as both small humans and cats watched the human with the deep voice get out of his truck and make his way to the porch door. Then, there would be a carefully choreographed dance where both porch door and sliding door needed to open and close simultaneously. Cats out – human with the deep voice in. The deep-voiced human pretended not to know the cats had been inside, so the game could continue another day.

Sure, a cat needed some alone time, but here, they found they most liked being with the small humans. The small humans spent time with them outside as well, and the two cats followed them everywhere. But their favourite place was behind the house in the trees the small humans called "the forest," where they held toy guns and imagined hunting big game, as the cats honed their own hunting skills.

When the weather turned colder, a warm house was built for them in the big barn across the road. A heat lamp kept them snug, and the old barn kept away the bitter winter winds. Riser and Dilly didn't mind the cold weather, and when it wasn't too cold and the small humans played outside, the cats would join them as they played in the snow. And so passed the first winter in their new home.

Spring came slowly that year, as it often does in the prairies, with teasing glimpses of warm weather followed by gusting winds and driving rain. Riser had grown into a sleek, handsome cat, his black stripes looking more tiger-ish as he aged. Dilly was a daintier version of her brother, with very similar body stripes, but her facial markings gave her a rather quizzical look, as if she was perpetually puzzled.

As she grew older, Dilly found she enjoyed an occasional solitary ramble without either the small humans or Riser. She could follow new smells at her leisure or take a new path of her own choosing. She found a secret delight in lying very still and watching the birds come almost within pouncing distance.

On one of these morning rambles, Dilly caught the faint whiff of something she had never smelled before. It was a cat, but there was another odour related to it as well. Cautiously, she padded along through the forest and came out into an open field. The wind gusted and almost blew the scent away, but as it died down, she picked it up again.

More confidently now, she trotted toward the closest grove of trees and stopped abruptly. A ginger cat with pale fur was lying on its side in the tall grass. One of its front paws was misshapen and bloody. The cat was very thin, and its flanks barely lifted with each of its shallow breaths.

Dilly crept closer to the injured cat, and as if it sensed her presence, it lifted its head slightly.

"What happened to your paw?" Dilly asked in alarm.

The ginger cat spoke so quietly that Dilly had to inch closer to hear. "I stepped on one of those traps that the humans put out to catch rats.

It was hidden under some weeds near that small barn. I got distracted by what I was hunting and wasn't watching where I stepped."

The effort of that much speech exhausted the thin cat, and his head sank back down. Pity for the thin, injured creature filled Dilly's warm heart. "Then what happened?" she encouraged.

"I tried to pry it off my paw, but that didn't work. So I had to chew the end of my foot off to get away."

Dilly was horrified. She felt an uncharacteristic sliver of anger toward humans enter her soul for the harm that had been done to this poor cat.

"What a horrible thing to happen to you! Who would do something like this to a cat?"

"You can't blame the humans – the trap wasn't meant for me. It was meant for the rats that are finding their way into the small barn. It was partly my fault for not paying attention. But I'm afraid it did some serious damage." The ginger cat looked sadly at his injured paw. The blood had congealed, and dirt and dried vegetation were stuck to the wound.

"When was the last time you ate?" Dilly asked, suddenly realizing the cat must be starving. "Clearly, you can't hunt right now." She continued with enthusiasm. "I'll go and get something for you from our dishes. Or I can hunt for you myself. Whatever you'd like."

The injured cat replied, "Maybe you'd better make it something from what the humans put out for you. From the looks of you, I don't think you do a lot of hunting."

Dilly bristled and drew herself up. "I will have you know I'm a good hunter! I can catch mice and sometimes birds, but I'd rather just watch the birds."

"We can debate your hunting skills later. Get me something to eat. Please?" The ginger cat looked at Dilly pleadingly; she realized the severity of the situation and nodded.

"I'll be back as soon as I can." She turned and ran quickly back to the house, skidding to a stop in front of the food dishes near the porch. They were empty. She was beginning to panic. The injured cat needed food. Then, she remembered she could ask the human for something more to eat.

Taking a deep breath, she leaped lightly onto the deck and then onto the railing underneath the window where the good cooking smells sometimes floated out. The window was open slightly, and she let out her most pathetic meow. There was no response. She tried again with a little more volume and pathos. The human appeared at the window, and very shortly, a pile of baked ham scraps dropped into their dishes. She gave the human a cursory rub around the ankles as a thank-you and then settled in as if she was going to eat it all.

The human disappeared back into the house, and as soon as she was gone, Dilly snatched the largest chunk of ham in her mouth and with her head held high, carried it swiftly back to the injured cat. He was dozing, and her arrival startled him.

"Well, what did you have to do to get that little tidbit?' he asked, his discomfort heightening his sarcasm.

"Nothing much," Dilly said proudly. "Just your basic 'Sit up, look cute, and sound sad.' Works every time." She laid the chunk of ham down near her new friend's nose. "Eat up. You need your strength."

The cat looked at the food incredulously. Staggering to his feet and swaying slightly, he sniffed it and then bolted it down. The effort exhausted him and he lay down again. He made a cursory attempt to wash his face, but it was hard to do with one paw lacerated and the other one needed for balance. It was a dismal failure.

Dilly saw him struggle with his grooming and asked, "May I?"

He nodded. Dilly stepped forward and began washing his face for him. The injured cat lifted his face in pleasure. A rumbly purr began deep in his chest. He hadn't had his face washed by another cat since his mother had done it for him.

"Thanks," he said gruffly.

Dilly nodded and continued her ministrations. The ginger cat's head dropped low and soon he was asleep. Dilly watched him, saddened at his plight and wondering how she could help him further. Then, she turned slowly and padded noiselessly back to the house.

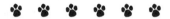

"Where were you?" Riser was right in her face, demanding answers.

"Relax. I just went for a walk. Nothing to see. Nothing new to smell. Boring really."

Eyes narrowed, Riser looked at his sister as if he didn't quite believe her. Dilly stepped onto their summer cushions, her mind full of questions as she kneaded their quilt to rearrange it for sleep. How was her new friend going to survive on his own? How was he going to heal without more help and more food? And if she didn't help him, who would?

Over the next few days, Dilly continued her covert operation to assist the injured cat. She waited until Riser had finished breakfast and gone to do his own exploring or was carried inside by the small humans. Then, she scooped up as much food as she could carry and headed straight to where the ginger cat lay.

The food Dilly brought *was* helping. The ginger cat felt his strength slowly returning, and his paw was starting to heal. One day, he found he could put a little weight on it. He was grateful for the help he was given, but as his health improved, he began to feel restless and trapped. To pass the time, he told Dilly stories about his life before he'd been injured. He described the thrill of wandering for miles, not knowing where he was going to sleep, the rush of a successful hunt, and the satisfaction of knowing he could depend on himself.

Dilly listened to his stories with fascination. The way the ginger cat described it, a feral lifestyle had many advantages and opportunities. She began to question her commitment to the home she had. She felt she would miss the small humans, yet in some way, her feelings toward humans had shifted on the day she realized a human-set trap could maim a cat.

But she couldn't go without telling Riser of her plans. He deserved to know how she felt and be spared the pain of never knowing what happened to her. And so, late one night, she told him everything – how she had found the injured cat, how she had been bringing him food, and how she wanted more than what the humans were offering.

Riser spat furiously, "Are you out of your mind? What do you think you're going to do when winter gets here and there's nowhere to sleep? Did you think about *that*? And how are you going to hunt in the snow? You don't know how to do that! And what about the small humans? Don't you think they'll miss you?"

Dilly answered quietly, "They might, but they'll have you. I know it's familiar and safe around here, but I just want to see other things. I want to –"

"I don't understand," Riser said, cutting her off angrily, his tail lashing. "I'll *never* understand! But I can see it's no use. Go then. *Go!*"

Dilly looked at her brother sadly. She wanted to leave without rancour, but that wasn't to be. Walking out of the garage for the last time, she looked over her shoulder at Riser. He turned his back on her and agitatedly kneaded the cushions. She took one last walk behind the house and looked up at the windows where the small humans slept; she remembered the comfort of their beds, their hugs, and their chatter. For a second, her resolution failed her. Then, she walked through the forest, head held high. This was to be her path. No turning back.

The morning after Dilly's departure, Riser found his anger had abated. In its place was sadness and loneliness.

She'll be back, he thought. *She doesn't know what she's doing.*

A week passed, and then a second one. The leaves were beginning to take on their fall colours, and there was a chill in the air when he awoke in the mornings.

Now that it's getting closer to winter, Riser thought, *she'll be back. She has to come back.*

I was used to Dilly's short absences, but when almost a month had passed and she hadn't returned, I began to wonder if something dire had befallen her.

Riser was despondent and terribly lonely. He needed company. A family friend was moving into a new home that would not allow animals, and her young cat with (in my friend's words) "a bit of an attitude" would need to be rehomed. I volunteered to take her pet, attitude and all. She was a beautiful calico with pale colours, thick fur, and as forewarned, a personality all of her own.

And so Angel came into our lives.

CHAPTER THREE

. . . .

ANGEL

*E*yes narrowed, Angel looked appraisingly at her new home. There were cushions in the open building before her, a healthy supply of kibble nearby, and from what the other resident of the place had grudgingly told her, a steady supply of tidbits from the human. She had been an indoor-outdoor cat in her former home, so living here would not be a major adjustment.

The other resident cat looked at her reproachfully. "You do know why you're here? It's because my sister left with a stray cat. But she's coming back. And when she does, you're going to have to leave."

Angel looked at him with disdain. "I don't think so, Stripey. You should have heard the way the human talked to me on the way here. *She* wants me, even if you don't. And by the way, I don't like how you've got those cushions arranged, and wouldn't it be better if –"

"The name isn't Stripey! It's Terrorizer. Maybe just think about that for a minute." Riser glared at her. "And the cushions are fine just the way they are!"

Whoa, Angel thought, taken aback. *Bit of an anger management problem, that one.*

She watched him cautiously as he hissed at her, the hair on his back rising and his tail lashing the dust on the garage floor. With an exasperated huff, he turned his back on her.

As he stalked away, Riser's irritation rose. Dilly's absence was still very painful. Yes, he was lonely, but he wanted *her.* Not some calico bimbo who thought she could take over the minute she got here. He padded away to the small barn, lost in thought, and began to pace back and forth. Mice rustled in the dry grass nearby, but he didn't hear them. The human was calling him, but he didn't hear her either.

This is all that stray cat's fault. I wish she'd just left him to die, Riser thought bitterly. *If she'd never seen him, she'd still be here.*

And thus was born a distrust of stray cats that would be passed down to all who came after him.

Back at the house, the small humans were smothering Angel with attention. *Back off, youngsters,* she thought crossly. *I'm not used to this, and I'm not sure if I really want to.*

She dashed under the car that brought her here, and watched with satisfaction as the small humans flopped down on their stomachs and tried to cajole her out. *Fat chance of that,* she thought triumphantly. *Leave me alone and I'll consider it later. Much, much later.*

The small humans eventually tired of their "Get Angel out!" game and moved on to other pursuits. Their shouts could be heard in the distance as they began a game in the other part of the yard.

Angel sighed in relief and carefully crawled out from under the car. Dust coated her fur, and she shook her head in dismay. How was a girl supposed to keep looking good when those two ruffians wanted to maul her and the only escape route was diving into dirt? She was beginning to wonder if this place *was* going to be a good fit for her.

And what about Stripey? she thought uneasily. *We didn't get off to a very good start. What if I won't be staying?* For a moment, her confidence wavered. *Who is this sister he was talking about?*

It was all too much to think about right now. A nap was definitely in order. She swayed sinuously toward the cushions in the garage, stopped for a dainty nibble of kibble, and then settled in – after arranging the cushions to her taste.

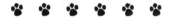

Over the next weeks, Riser and Angel reached an uneasy truce. Riser was losing hope that Dilly was coming back, whether through choice or misfortune. And he realized that, if he wanted companionship, Angel was all there was. There was no way he was going to befriend a stray cat. However, he couldn't understand Angel's aversion to the small humans, whom he adored.

For her part, in the spirit of cooperation, Angel tried to see some redeeming features in them. But, try as she might, she just couldn't. The small humans were obnoxiously loud, they were always in her face, they chased her around the yard, and when they caught her and picked her up (which she abhorred), they messed up her fur. She could tolerate the human who brought her here, because one had to put up with those who fed you and sheltered you, but the others? Not a chance.

One afternoon, when the first snowflakes were coming down and looking as if they were here to stay, the human with the deep voice began the process of constructing their winter home.

"What on earth is all of *that*?" Angel asked in horror, as a tractor pulled into the yard with their home-building equipment in its bucket.

"It's going to be our new winter home," Riser replied. "What? Not classy enough for you? It might not look like much, but it'll be warm and safe."

I'll just reserve my judgement on that *point,* Angel thought sourly, as she watched the human with the deep voice begin the process. Riser left her side to oversee the construction. He nodded his head at the positioning of the straw bales, he agreed with the addition of an extra heat lamp, and he heartily approved of the quilt brought out by the human to cover the winter cushions.

When construction was complete and the quilt arranged, Riser padded inside. His voice was muffled as he called, "Come on in and check it out! You'll like it!"

"I doubt that very much," Angel muttered, "but I don't see that there's going to be a lot of choice here." She walked slowly over to the winter home's opening. Inside, Riser was stretched out full-length, absorbing the warmth of the heat lamps overhead. He appeared to be half-asleep already. Stepping around him, Angel settled toward the back of the enclosure.

Not bad, she admitted grudgingly, looking around at the thick walls. *Not bad at all.*

Riser murmured sleepily, "And when the weather gets really miserable, the human will probably bring food right out here. We won't even have to go out in the cold." A thought struck him, and he lifted his head to glare at Angel. "Except to do our business. Don't *ever* do that in here!"

Angel rolled her eyes. As if a lady would ever do anything like that. "Agreed." The warmth from the lamps *was* exceptionally nice, and Angel admired the way their warm ruby glow highlighted the shine on her fur.

I could get used to this, she thought with satisfaction.

That opinion was confirmed with the arrival of a warm breakfast the next morning and for many days to follow. The winter was a bitter one, with constant snow and biting winds. There would be occasional days of milder weather, when both cats could enjoy the feeble sun on their fur, but those days were rare. The human checked on them often to make sure they were warm and well.

There's one good thing about this miserable weather, Angel thought wryly. *At least those small humans aren't pestering the life out of me.*

And if inside the house, they wouldn't be able to use the insulting new nickname they'd chosen for her: Mange.

As the winter slowly passed, Riser and Angel grew closer, occasionally even cuddling together on especially frigid nights. She stopped calling him Stripey, which was a relief, and he stopped poking fun at her occasionally condescending attitude. He almost broke that resolution on the day Angel was showing off her agility by climbing on the garage shelves near their heated water bowl, slipped, and fell in. When she stood up, completely drenched, she looked half her size. Spitting with anger, she stomped off to the warm winter home to dry off. Riser followed her with amusement in his eyes.

"Not a word. Do you hear me? *Not. A. Word."* She glared at him, her skinny, water-soaked tail lashing in fury. Her fur was plastered to her body; with a sigh of resignation, she began the lengthy process of a full-body grooming. "Look at this mess! I *hate* getting wet. And eeewww… look at the stuff that must have been in the bottom of the water bowl." She scowled and plucked some larger pieces of debris from her fur.

Riser sat down beside her and began to assist. She looked at him in astonishment. "Why are you helping me?"

"Why not? I'm not going anywhere in this weather, and you have to get dried off or you'll get chilled. And if you get chilled, you could get sick. And I really don't want to have to get used to another cat…" he paused briefly, "…now that I've got used to you."

Angel was speechless. Riser refused to look up, apparently engrossed in removing a stubborn bit of grime from her shoulder. Together, they worked quietly to remove all traces of water and dirt. When they had finished, they curled up together under the heat lamps and drifted off to sleep.

Despite all evidence to the contrary, winter on the prairies does eventually end. The days lengthened, and the sun crept higher in the sky. The snow slowly sank away, and the summer birds returned.

After her winter of confinement, Angel felt restless. Granted, Riser had become an acceptable companion, and they were rarely at odds with one another. But she was feeling the need to prowl – to go somewhere – to experience something new. Riser didn't understand her urge to roam. Over and over again, he did his best to relay his fears about roaming and the possible influence of stray cats.

Riser could see he was fighting a losing battle. And one afternoon, while he was comfortably ensconced in the house with the small humans, Angel walked off through their forest, between the taller rows of trees, and down a new path that wound around a shallow pond of water. Carefully avoiding the water, she followed the path, which had been trod by countless feet. Numerous smells emanated from it: mice, voles, rabbits, and, she noted with interest, other cats.

True outdoor cats smell different, she thought with her nose to the ground. The smell was both repulsive and compelling. One particular scent caught her attention. She could smell it on a variety of dried grasses and near trees. The scent was taking her away from Riser and the house and all of the things she knew, but she didn't care. The scent was the only thing that mattered.

Minutes or maybe hours later – she didn't know – Angel emerged into a clearing. She could smell water nearby, and she was thirsty from her travels. She stepped carefully down to a creek and bent her head to drink. The water was icy-cold and delicious.

As she drank, Angel had the feeling she was being observed. She lifted her head, water dripping from her chin. A large, dark grey, long-haired cat was lounging nearby, watching her lazily. Taking a deep breath, Angel realized it was his scent she'd been following. His fur was dappled in the shade, and his eyes never left hers.

She stared at him as he rose to his feet, stretched, and padded slowly toward her. As he came closer, Angel could see that his fur had silvery highlights. His mesmerizing green eyes glittered with intent. He touched her nose with his and then moved behind her. He sank his teeth into the skin on the back of her neck. She could feel his weight on her back. Before she knew what was happening, it was over.

The grey cat released her neck and, without a second glance, walked lazily away. Dazed, Angel watched him go. She got to her feet, and shook off the dirt and bits of grass that clung to her fur. Then silently, she turned toward home.

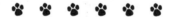

The walk home was endless. Without the exhilaration of following that strange, wonderful, awful scent, Angel realized she was exhausted. It was dark before she crawled into the garage and collapsed onto the summer cushions. She ached everywhere. Riser was nowhere to be seen.

His Lordship is probably still lounging in the house, she thought disgustedly. She was hungry but couldn't get up to eat. She was desperately thirsty yet didn't want to drink.

Darkness closed in around her. Riser still wasn't back. He couldn't have been in the house because Angel had heard the human with the deep voice come home a long time ago. Just as she was slipping into sleep, she heard Riser pad into the garage. She felt the cushions shift as he settled in beside her.

"Where were you?" she asked acidly.

"No, the question is: where were *you?*" Riser shot back.

"I was just out exploring, and then I found a smell that I had to follow. I can't explain it. At first, I didn't realize how far away I was, and then when I did, I came back," she concluded lamely. There was a long pause. She could tell that Riser didn't entirely believe her explanation, but he chose not to argue with her.

"Well, I'm glad you came back." Gruffly, he added, "Better get some sleep – it's getting really late." He curled in closer, kneaded the cushions briefly, and gave a contented sigh. Soon, his gentle purrs reverberated against her.

Angel lay awake for a long time. Upon reflection, she realized she had an instinctive understanding of the events of the afternoon, but it was all too much to think about right now. She rose and left the cushions for a drink of water and then curled up beside Riser. Soon, her purrs joined his.

Angel's understanding of that afternoon's events proved correct. In a few weeks, she felt a faint stirring of new life deep in her body. To her dismay, she lost her kittenish figure. She was always tired and constantly hungry, and turned her frustration on Riser, who was undeserving of her wrath.

"Just *look* at me!" she wailed one warm afternoon. "I look like I swallowed two whole squirrels. I can't fit through the openings on the deck anymore. My back hurts, and if I get any bigger, my belly will be dragging on the ground!"

Riser turned away to hide his amusement. "Look, it won't last forever. I mean, I don't know how much bigger you *can* get before you explode. How many do you think you have in there? Ten? Twelve?"

Angel waddled off the cushions and tried to get comfortable in front of the water bowl. It was impossible, so she contented herself by dipping a paw in and licking off the water. Between licks, she asked plaintively, "Could you do me a favour? Scrape that pile of kibble up higher so I don't have to bend down so far?"

Riser did as he was asked. He watched as Angel pushed herself away from the water dish and tried to find a comfortable position to eat.

When that didn't work, she stretched out beside the kibble, pulled a nugget over, and nibbled it listlessly. Riser watched her, concern replacing his initial amusement. She *was* huge – what if she had problems having the kittens? What was he going to do then? And what did the human know about having kittens?

His worries proved groundless. Two days later, while the human and the small humans were all away from the house, Angel lay inside a cardboard box in the garage and gave birth to two tiny kittens. Riser stood by anxiously and helplessly as she laboured. But it all happened quickly. By the time the humans arrived home, Angel hopped out of the box and proudly directed them toward her new family, even submitting graciously to some congratulatory pats from the small humans.

Riser found, to his absolute delight, that he loved the new kittens. He loved the way they smelled, he loved to watch them push their tiny paws into Angel's belly as they nursed, and he loved to watch them sleep. Her family had become his family. And he promised himself he would do whatever was necessary to protect them.

We were delighted with the new kittens and had the joyful task of coming up with names for them. The little male had a face like a full moon, along with soft grey tabby colours. He was named MoonMan but promptly nicknamed Moonsie. The little female was dappled with bright calico colours and had distinctive black markings around her eyes, like a little mask. She was named Bandit.

And without any effort on our part, Moonsie and Bandit came into our lives.

CHAPTER FOUR

....

MOONSIE AND BANDIT

"*Slow down!*" Bandit exclaimed. "You're getting too far ahead of me! Don't you remember? Riser said we're always supposed to go together."

Moonsie snorted impatiently. "Awww, he's just an old worrywart. We'll be fine. And it isn't like we're going *away*. We're going *up!*"

Moonsie loved to climb. And he would climb anything: tractor tires, deck railings, vehicles – although that was a bit more of a challenge, as it was difficult to sink his claws into chrome. But his all-time favourite climbing objects were trees. From the time he was first able to sink his tiny claws into tree bark, he was hooked. The only problem was he wasn't quite as agile getting down. Now, *that* took a lot more coordination, a quality he did not yet possess in abundance.

Moonsie had his eyes set on a scolding squirrel, who always managed to leap a few tantalizing inches ahead of him and could balance on the slenderest of twigs. He hadn't paid attention to how high he was climbing and suddenly found himself in a precarious situation.

From her position much farther down, Bandit called, "What's wrong? Are you stuck?"

Moonsie looked down briefly and lied. "Nope, just taking a little rest." His quick glance confirmed what he'd feared: he had climbed much higher than he should have and his path down was going to be very difficult. The ground looked far below him, and Bandit appeared to be half her normal size.

"You'd better start coming down," Bandit called again, more anxiously this time. Despite not wanting to admit defeat, Moonsie felt a hint of anxiety.

Why can't I just leave those squirrels alone? he thought ruefully. *And why do they have to tease me? One day, I'm going to give it to them.*

But not today. Moonsie realized he was going to have to turn around on the branch. Fortunately, there were tiny twigs on both sides of it. Using those twigs, and trying not to put too much weight on anything, Moonsie turned himself by tiny degrees and got pointed in the right direction.

Bandit cried enthusiastically, "That's good – good! Keep going!"

Buoyed by her confidence, Moonsie moved a little too quickly. The next thing he knew, he had both front paws wrapped around the branch while his back feet dangled helplessly in the air.

Bandit comprehended the severity of the situation immediately. "I'm going to get Riser! You can't do this by yourself!" She dropped to the ground from her much-lower position and ran swiftly in the direction of the summer cushions.

Oh, this is just great, Moonsie thought. *I can't wait to hear what he's going to say about* this. His grip on the branch was beginning to loosen, and despite his sarcasm, he was terrified. He let out a pitiful meow.

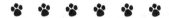

Bandit tore back to the summer cushions as if her tail was on fire. *Riser, I need Riser,* she thought in panic. *Please, please, be there.*

She skidded to a stop in front of the garage. Riser was in the middle of his morning grooming session. Angel was nowhere to be seen. She had been taken away in the carrier by the human earlier that morning. Riser suspected the human knew about Angel's roaming tendencies and was as concerned about it as he was. He also suspected that where Angel was going would take care of *that*.

"Riser, Moonsie's up a tree again and I think he's going to fall! You have to come and get him down!"

Riser was off the cushions before Bandit had finished her breathless speech. "Where is he?" he asked tersely.

"Through the forest, in the first row of trees. You'll hear him before you see him!"

Riser was equally terrified and furious. How many times had he told that little grey rip to be careful and not get into situations he didn't have the strength or maturity to get out of? His fear lent him speed and he was at the base of the tree Moonsie was clinging to before Bandit had even cleared the forest. Riser shot up the tree and was beside Moonsie in seconds.

The kitten was shaking now, and Riser could see he was nearing the end of his strength.

"Now, look at me. *Look. At. Me*," Riser commanded quietly. Moonsie pulled his terrified gaze from the ground and turned his head. "I'm going to stand below you on that branch" – Riser gestured with a paw – "and you can rest your back feet on me and then push yourself up. Understand?"

Moonsie nodded once. Riser carefully positioned himself on the branch below him. Arching his back as high as he could, Riser watched over his shoulder as one of Moonsie's back feet got a purchase in his fur. The kitten pushed off Riser's back and hooked his paw onto the branch. Seconds later, all four paws were solidly anchored.

"Now, here's what you do. Keep coming slowly toward the trunk. When you get there, reach around it with both front paws as far as you can and hang on. Your back paws will automatically swing around and then you can catch onto the trunk with all four feet. Got it?" Riser's directions were calm and precise.

Moonsie nodded again. Carefully, he inched toward the trunk and stretched his small paws around it as far as he could reach. Riser waited until Moonsie's small bottom swung around and clung to the trunk; he leaped off the branch he was standing on and secured himself to the trunk a little below Moonsie. Together, they backed slowly toward the ground, Riser ready to act as a cushion if necessary. Once on the ground, the older cat's anxiety gave way immediately to anger.

"*How many times?* How many times do I have to tell you you're not ready to be climbing like this? You could have killed yourself!"

Back on the ground with his breathing returning to normal, Moonsie realized Riser was right. He *had* gone too high without paying attention, and he *could* have hurt himself very badly. He hung his head with shame as Riser's tirade continued. Bandit crept up beside him. He could feel her sympathy as she leaned in and quietly groomed the fur on the side of his face.

Finally, Riser stopped for breath. He wilted visibly and said quietly to both kittens, "Come here." Bandit left her brother's side and cuddled close to Riser. Moonsie glanced up sheepishly. He and Riser considered one other, and slowly, Moonsie padded over and buried his face in the older cat's warm fur. With a sigh, Riser pulled Moonsie closer to him.

"I just don't want you to get hurt. If you want to climb taller trees, do it when I'm around so I can help you figure out the best way to do it. Can we agree on that?"

Moonsie nodded.

"And all of this goes for you, too!" Riser said, pulling back so he could look at Bandit directly. She was all wide-eyed innocence.

"*Me?* I don't even like climbing trees all that much. You don't have to worry about me causing trouble!"

We shall see, Riser thought cynically.

Cats, like humans, can go through long periods of time without either major adventures or catastrophes. Life goes on quietly with little dramas, such as throwing up after eating flowers in the deck pots or falling into the trash barrel, not really being worth mentioning.

Summer faded into fall, and fall cooled into winter. Winter finally gave way to spring, and the cycle began again. Fall's transformation into winter that year was very gradual. There were warm sunny days that almost felt summer-like, followed by days that hinted at snow to come.

As he grew older, Moonsie found he liked being close to home. And home, to him, meant Riser. Moonsie realized that the older cat had a great understanding of many things. They went for long prowls together, and while they prowled, Riser told him stories about when he and Dilly were kittens and what it was like to be a house cat.

One mild afternoon, the two cats took a stroll down to the creek. The water was very low, and because the weather was so unseasonably warm, the creek had not yet frozen. Riser found a branch that had fallen over a narrow segment of the creek and crossed it with ease. He beckoned for Moonsie to follow him.

Moonsie skillfully made his way over the branch, landing lightly on the other side. The two cats climbed the opposite creek bank, weaving around fallen branches. At the top, they could see a neighbouring farm site in the distance. Riser knew of its existence, and even though he rarely wandered that far from home, he knew that many cats lived there. Some of them were permanent residents, sheltered during the winter and fed all year long. Others were more transient, staying briefly to feed and then vanishing.

Riser continued onward, but Moonsie balked, suddenly wary. "What are we doing? You've never taken me this way before. Aren't we getting a little far away from home?"

"It's fine. I've been this way before. There's nothing to worry about." Riser gestured with his paw. "Come on."

Despite his misgivings, Moonsie followed. The two cats padded quietly through a harvested field, the soil cool beneath their feet. Overhead, late-flying flocks of geese honked discordantly. The sun held some warmth, but when clouds passed over, the temperature dropped.

Moonsie shivered. "What's on your mind? You must have some reason for wanting to go this way today."

Riser was slow to reply. He padded on ahead of Moonsie and then sat down to examine a small thorn in his paw.

"I just wondered if any of those cats who live over there" – he tilted his head toward the farm site – "had any idea about Dilly, if they'd seen her or knew what happened to her. Just because I don't talk about her all the time doesn't mean I've forgotten her."

"I don't think that will do much good. She's been gone for a long time now and chances are she's likely –"

"Don't," Riser snapped. "I don't want to hear it." He bent over his paw, nipped out the painful thorn, and tossed it aside. "It's just something I've been thinking about for a while." He licked at the tender spot briefly and then stood up.

Moonsie shook his head. This was a hopeless journey if ever he heard of one. But where Riser went, he would follow. He was afraid, though, that Riser would have his heart broken once and for all. Maybe it was better not to know for sure. Uncertainty left a little hope.

The two cats continued in the direction of the farm, leaving the harvested field for a narrow dirt road. At the end of the road was the farm, which consisted of a small, run-down barn, a weather-beaten house, and a pair of small sheds. Riser trotted directly to the barn and, after examining the base for an entrance point, slipped inside where one of the wooden slats had splintered and lifted.

Moonsie followed him, squeezing carefully through the broken slat. It took a little time for his eyes to get used to the gloom, but eventually he could see many cats of all different colours and sizes. Some were perched on rotting straw bales; others were engaged in varying aspects of grooming while kittens chased one another in play. He didn't know so many cats could live in one place and be looked after by one human. It was astonishing.

Riser padded over the straw-covered floor where a large white and grey female with bright green eyes was nibbling at some scraps. He stopped at a respectful distance and waited.

The female lifted her head. She and Riser looked at each other guardedly.

"I'm not here to cause trouble," Riser began.

"I believe you," the female replied. "I've seen you near here. You don't seem like the sort to start a fight." She stared levelly at Riser. "So why *are* you here?"

"I know this will sound foolish but I wondered if you, or any of the cats around here, had seen my littermate. She looks a lot like me, just smaller. She left our home quite a while ago because she had befriended an injured stray cat, and he talked her into going away with him." Riser's bitterness became more evident as his explanation progressed.

"Chances are they're miles away from here. You know that, right?" the female stated quietly.

"I know. I knew it was a long shot. I just wondered if she had possibly changed her mind and come here to live with all of you." Riser hung his head.

"If she was here, why would she not have gone back home?"

"I don't know. Pride. Fear. Both." Riser turned dejectedly and then abruptly swung around. "But if you do ever see her, just tell her she can come home."

The female nodded, and her eyes remained on him as he walked slowly back to the broken slat and slipped out. Moonsie followed him. He had countless questions but sensed that now was not the time to ask. The sun was beginning to drop in the sky as they walked quietly down the dirt road, back to the harvested field, and began retracing their footsteps toward home.

"*Wait, wait!*" A small, sleek ginger cat sped toward them, raising a small cloud of dust when he skidded to a stop. "I think I know the cat you were talking about." Breathlessly, he added, "She was my mother."

Riser couldn't believe what he was hearing. He knew going over to the other farm was a long shot, and he hadn't really thought anything would come of it. But now! If this cat was telling the truth...

"What makes you think my littermate was your mother?" he asked skeptically.

"She looked a lot like you. She told me my father had the same colours as me, and he had a front paw that had been hurt. She said it made him walk funny sometimes."

"Where is she now? Tell me, *tell me!*"

The cat dropped his gaze, refusing to meet Riser's eyes. "One day, when we were out hunting, a coyote tracked us. There was nowhere for us to run. She kept the coyote away from me so I could escape. Later, I went back to look for her, but she was dead. There was so much blood..." The little cat closed his eyes and took a deep breath.

"I was so scared and I didn't know what to do. I just walked and walked and one day, I found the barn with all the cats. And I've been here ever since."

At the other cat's words, Riser felt his whole world shift. He wished he'd never come over here. He wished he'd tried harder to convince Dilly to stay. He wished he didn't know. He wished it had been him lying dead in a field.

Moonsie said haltingly, "Thank you for telling us. I'm really sorry about your mother."

The little cat nodded. "I'm sorry too. I know that's not what you wanted to hear." He looked up at the darkening sky. "I'd better get back." He looked at Riser, opened his mouth as if to say something else, then closed it and trotted away.

Moonsie moved close beside Riser. "Come on," he said quietly. "We need to go home." Silently, the two cats padded through the harvested field, the soil now cold beneath their feet. The birds had stopped singing. The sun had almost set.

Bandit, like her mother, loved to roam. However, her purpose in roaming was entirely different than her mother's. She roamed in order to hunt. And she loved to hunt.

Bandit's skills as a hunter were steadily improving. As a kitten, she was a successful hunter of insects. Grasshoppers, half-dead on the front of the human's car, were a favourite treat as well as an easy catch. Now, as a fully grown cat, she could see the extra benefits in being a skilled hunter. Any prey brought back to the human received exuberant praise. Thus, Bandit made it a habit to bring back her catch, unless of course, it was a tasty treat that required immediate consumption.

On the same warm fall afternoon Moonsie was accompanying Riser on his grim errand, Bandit set off on a solo hunt. Today, she was out to bag big game. Today's quarry was… a squirrel.

Dozens of squirrels lived in the treetops of the forest. Chattering and scolding, they taunted not only her but any cat walking below them. They were mouthy and rude, and if only she could get her paws on one – there would be justice! She had gotten close to one before, a juvenile incautious enough to loiter on the ground longer than it should. Just as Bandit had pounced, the squirrel gave a saucy twitch of its tail and scampered up a tree. All she had to show for her pains that day were a few long red tail hairs caught in her front claws.

But not today, because Bandit had a plan. She knew that a few squirrels sunned themselves on these lazy late-fall afternoons on a fallen, moss-covered log in the forest. She knew this fact, because she'd watched them from a distance on more than one occasion.

The weather: perfect.

The wind: in the right direction.

The hunter: on point.

The prey: about to go down.

Bandit crept into the edge of the forest, taking great care to watch where every soft footfall landed. She used the trees as cover, the fallen branches as camouflage. Closer, closer…

A blue jay squawked raucously, signalling her presence. The squirrels, distracted by the bird's call, looked in its direction. It was Bandit's opportunity, and she took it. Using all the considerable strength in her back legs, she leaped for the squirrel nearest her. She caught it by the tail and quickly sank her teeth into the loose skin around its neck. Apparently, her teeth hit something vital, as the squirrel immediately went limp, its body flopping in her mouth.

Well, that wasn't so hard at all, she thought victoriously. "But you're a lot heavier than you look," she said, through a mouthful of fluffy, surprisingly irritating fur.

Carrying, but mostly dragging, her amazing catch, Bandit made her halting way back to the house, the squirrel's limp body feeling heavier with each step. She could already hear the effusive praise her grateful human would heap on her. She and she alone was the killer of squirrels – the eliminator of one of these infernal pests. She quickened her pace, accidentally on purpose thwacking the squirrel's head on the corner of the garage.

Bandit heaved her catch up the deck steps and, with a grateful sigh, dropped it in front of the sliding door. The squirrel was looking more than a little dishevelled, its shiny red fur covered in dust, dead leaves, and dry grass.

For all the smack they talk, they sure die easy, Bandit thought smugly as she looked at its motionless body.

She meowed to attract the human's attention. She could hear a roaring sound inside the house and watched as the human dragged some sort of machine back and forth across the floor. The roaring stopped and Bandit meowed again, louder this time. To make doubly sure she was seen, she stretched up on her hind legs and pawed at the glass.

The human hurried over to the sliding door and wrenched it open. She leaned out over the squirrel and stroked Bandit's head and back, again and again, giving her tail gentle tugs. Bandit writhed with ecstasy.

This is living, she thought. *A successful hunt and a human who adores me. How could it possibly get any better?*

The squirrel opened one beady black eye…

Calculating his next move, the squirrel lay as still as possible, slowing down his breathing through sheer force of will. He watched through lowered eyelids as the ridiculous cat turned cartwheels for the human.

Does it really think we squirrels give up so easily? he thought contemptuously. The bigger question, however, was… how was he going to get out of this predicament? He thought through his options.

Plan A. *I'll zip through the slats in the deck and straight up the bird-feeder tree.*

Problem with Plan A. *I'll get caught as there's nowhere to go after the top of the bird-feeder tree.*

Plan B. *I'll jump onto the deck railing and make a mad leap onto the roof of the house.*

Problem with Plan B. *I'm barking mad if I think I can leap onto the roof of the house.*

Plan C. *What if I bolt under the human's legs into the house, cause maximum confusion, and then bolt out the door again?*

Problem with Plan C. *No problem. Yeah, right.*

Bandit watched in disbelief as her prize catch leaped to its feet and shot through the open sliding door into the house. The human shrieked. Bandit tore into the house after the wretch. The squirrel ricocheted off furniture and leaped onto countertops. Houseplants were overturned, photographs knocked off shelves, and books and papers scattered as squirrel and cat raced through the unprotected house with mad abandon, accompanied by continued and hysterical shrieking by the human.

After scaling a tall cabinet, the squirrel took a second to catch his breath and consider his next move. If he timed it *just* right, he should be able to shoot onto that big table and springboard right out the open door. He took a deep breath…

Leap. Another gigantic leap. Ahhhh, freedom.

All Bandit saw of her prize catch was a twitch of its wretched saucy tail as the squirrel zipped down the deck steps.

The human stopped shrieking and fell into a chair, surveying the damage. Bandit crawled wearily out the sliding door and collapsed onto the deck, infuriated she had, yet again, been bested by one of those mouthy furry things. Apparently, there was to be no justice where squirrels were concerned.

She was still sulking on the deck as Riser and Moonsie arrived home. But she could tell by their dejected appearance – tails down and heads hanging low – that something was indeed very wrong.

She met them at the summer cushions and waited. Riser said nothing; for the first time, he looked like an old cat as he climbed onto the cushions and curled into a tight ball. With a subtle tilt of his head, Moonsie gestured for Bandit to follow him. They left the garage and walked a short distance out into the forest.

"Where were you two? You were gone a long time," Bandit whispered.

"I'll tell you the whole story later, but for right now, all you need to know is Dilly is dead."

"I guess we likely knew that, but it's still awful. Poor Riser..."

"I know. He won't want to talk about it for a while, maybe not ever. We'll just have to respect his wishes about it."

Bandit nodded. Together, they crept back into the garage. Bandit stepped carefully onto the cushions and gently wrapped her paws around Riser's shivering form. Moonsie cuddled down next to them both.

Riser could feel their unspoken sympathy and was comforted by their presence. Eventually, they slept.

The seasons passed. Moonsie and Bandit had left kittenhood behind them long ago. No one left the comfort of the cushions to hunt, and all four cats remained close to home. Angel's colours were fading; Moonsie had experienced some difficulties with his ears, which affected his hearing while Bandit's amber eyes held vision-clouding brown spots. Even though he was the oldest of the lot, Riser still felt responsible for the other cats' safety and well-being.

One winter night, as all four cats were curled together in their winter home, Riser thought he could hear the sound of footfalls in the snow. As the sound got closer, he extricated himself from the other cats and stood quietly at the entrance, looking out. In the moonlight, he could see two large, shaggy, white dogs trotting down the road almost directly across from the winter home, destination unknown. Uneasily, he watched them as they continued around the bend and out of sight.

What are they doing up here? he wondered. The dogs were supposed to be down with the livestock they were brought there to guard, not roaming at will. The appearance of the dogs spooked him. He lay awake for the rest of the night, watching over the other cats.

In the morning, he told Angel about what he'd seen. She was unconcerned and told him there was nothing wrong with the dogs going on a little adventure. In fact, she envied them.

"At least, they still have the motivation to get out and go somewhere. Mine is all gone," she said wistfully.

"Well, maybe they're not out to cause problems, but I still don't trust them," Riser responded quietly, not wishing to alarm the two younger cats.

The next night, the dogs appeared again. This time, they stopped and sniffed near the cats' winter home. Riser rose to his feet, barring the entrance; he snarled and hissed at them, and they backed away in mild astonishment.

The smaller of the two dogs growled deep in his chest, curling his lip and baring his teeth in a menacing snarl. He stepped closer to the entrance of the winter home, staring at Riser. His eyes were ice-cold. Riser felt a frisson of fear race down his spine. He swallowed his panic and with great difficulty, maintained eye contact with the huge animal.

The second, larger dog shouldered her companion aside, and in one smooth motion, she pulled out the cats' food dish and rapidly inhaled the remaining supper scraps. With a long, pink tongue, she swiped the plate clean.

With his heart pounding, Riser stood his ground as the shaggy female brought her nose within inches of his. Then, as swiftly as they'd come, both dogs turned and trotted back out to the road and past the bridge to the sheep they had left unattended.

Angel had awakened at the sound of their supper dish being roughly dragged out into the snow. With her heart pounding and panic rising, she forced herself to remain motionless. As the dogs finally trotted away, she rose on shaky legs to stand beside Riser.

"Again? What do you think they want?"

Riser found he could breathe again and replied, "I wish it was only scraps." Turning back into the enclosure, he pushed his head against Moonsie and then Bandit. "Come on, you two, wake up."

Bandit raised her head sleepily. "What's wrong?" Moonsie opened one eye blearily.

"It's those dogs from the farm across the bridge. They're dangerous; I feel sure of it. We're going to have to start spending nights down in the big barn."

Bandit whined, "But we don't have heat lamps down there. And the human won't bring food down and what about –"

"A heat lamp and food deliveries aren't going to matter a whole lot if you're dead, are they?" Riser snapped.

All three cats stared at him. He continued, "So, here's what we're going to do. We'll come up in the morning and evening for meals, but the rest of the time, we'll be in the big barn. It won't be as comfortable, but there are lots of places to hide. And even if the dogs did smell us down there, they won't be able to get to us."

The other cats finally agreed with his plan, and following Riser's footprints in the deep snow, they wove their way down to the old barn. Inside, they found a sheltered and relatively comfortable area bedded with old straw. Curling up together, three cats drifted off to sleep.

Riser dozed fitfully. In his dreams, the huge white beasts were coming closer, their jaws snapping at his heels. Dilly's heels. They were coming closer, closer… they were closing in on –

His head snapped up. He looked around in panic, and then realized the other three cats were still nestled beside him. His breathing slowed, and then he, too, slept.

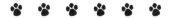

Riser's plan worked. Every morning and evening, the cats would come up for meals and then quickly return to the barn. After every breakfast, Riser would sniff around the winter home, checking for any fresh traces of the dogs. Days passed, and there was no evidence they'd been back. The other cats began to get complacent, napping in the shelter during the day and resisting when Riser told them it was time to go back to the barn in the evening.

Riser sensed he was fighting a losing battle. And he was tired of the fight. He hated to admit it, but he was just tired. Period. And so, the cats returned to their winter home. Riser acknowledged that the heat lamps were soothing to his aching body. Their time in the barn had taken its toll on all of them.

The nights were uneventful. Riser began to let down his guard, thinking the dogs were no longer a threat or perhaps they were actually doing their job, chasing the coyotes away from the sheep they were there to guard.

But one bitingly cold late-winter night, his worst fears became reality.

The full moon illuminated the stark winter landscape. Quickly and quietly, the two dogs trotted from the sheep farm, across the bridge, and toward the winter home where the four cats slept.

Moonsie was the first to scent danger. Sleeping nearest the doorway, his head snapped up as the two dogs stood at the entrance of the enclosure, deep growls emanating from their chests, lips curled, and teeth bared.

"Riser... *Riser!*" he whispered frantically. Riser lifted his head. In his soul, he knew this was his last night on earth.

The next few minutes passed at light speed yet seemed to happen in slow motion. With her teeth and paws, the vicious shaggy female tore at the side of the enclosure. Within seconds, the side wall was torn down.

"*Run!*" Riser hissed at the other cats. He faced the female with his back arched and his ears flattened. He flew at the dog with his claws outstretched and slashed her across the nose.

She yelped in surprise and pain. Her hesitancy gave the other three cats an opportunity to escape. Floundering in the deep snow, they struggled to the nearest trees and raced up. The second dog, enraged at their escape, lunged at the trees again and again in a frenzied attempt to reach them. The three cats watched in horror as Riser tried desperately to join them, but the female's snapping jaws caught his back foot. He struggled to break free, turning to slash at her again with his claws.

Riser fought for his life with all his strength, but he was no match for adversaries that outweighed him many times over. The female's powerful jaws clamped down on his throat. His lifeless body was shaken violently and then thrown down in the snow. Having accomplished their mission, the dogs made their way home, muzzles bathed in blood.

Angel, Moonsie, and Bandit clung to the tree branches for the rest of that endless freezing night. At dawn, they crept stiffly down and made their way slowly back to the wreckage of their winter home. One of the heat lamps swung crazily on its cord, and snow from the roof had fallen in on their quilt. The rank smell of dog was everywhere. Shivering, they stole down to the old barn, where they huddled together, still in shock.

A little later, the human with the deep voice came outdoors. As he rounded the corner of the house, he could see the wreckage of the cats' winter home, and a little farther away, he could see a bloody patch in the snow. With a heavy heart, he approached what he knew was the dead body of one of the cats.

He knelt in the snow, stroking Riser's lifeless body. Rage at the senselessness and cruelty of the old cat's death filled him. He gently picked Riser up and laid him carefully in the back of his truck, then walked slowly toward the house to deliver what he knew would be devastating news.

My heart broke for Riser and the manner in which he died. No cat deserved to have his life ended in that way. He was a beautiful cat with a gentle soul, and his death was a desecration. And how much of what happened was my fault? I knew the dogs were roaming. I knew they were a possible threat. And I didn't do nearly enough to protect him — to protect all of them. His death taught me that it should never be wrong to advocate for the safety of those you love.

In the spring after Riser's death, my niece offered me a kitten. Her cat had had a large litter, and she knew the kitten would have a good home. But was it? What kind of home was I offering where a cat could not be assured of safety?

Despite my misgivings, I told her I would take the kitten. He was a dapper little tuxedo with white paws, a white dickey, and a charming little white splotch on one side of his face. I loved him on sight.

And so Chuck came into our lives.

CHAPTER FIVE

. . . .

CHUCK

Moonsie was devastated after Riser's horrific death. And he felt guilty. He should have done more to help him. As always, Riser's concern had been for the three of them. Moonsie knew, even if he had come to Riser's aid, that it wouldn't have made a difference. They stood no chance against those dogs. The outcome would have been the same, and both if not all of the cats would have died.

Angel, Moonsie, and Bandit spent the remainder of the winter in the old barn. The human with the deep voice dismantled the ruins of the winter home, as it was clear the cats were no longer safe there. The human did her best to comfort them, coming down to the old barn regularly, bringing them food, and sitting in the straw with them. Moonsie could tell she was grieving the loss of Riser as well. He would sit on her lap, and he could tell that, even though she was stroking him, she was thinking of Riser.

The cats avoided the spot where their winter home had been. It brought back too many memories, and it still smelled of dogs and death. But spring rains came, and time passed. The rains washed away the smells, and the sense of grief brought by Riser's loss eased. Warm breezes from the south brought no scent of dog or any sound of their barking. There was no scent of the sheep they had been brought there to protect. The cats began to feel as if they were finally safe.

One morning, the human drove away with the carrier in her car. Moonsie watched her leave with trepidation. None of them were in the carrier, so did that mean someone was coming back with her?

His supposition was correct. The human returned later in the day, and inside the carrier was a small kitten. He was black, with tiny white paws and vivid white whiskers. The human set the carrier down in the garage, leaving its door closed, and returned to the house.

Apparently, she doesn't want to let it out, Bandit thought anxiously.

It will never replace Riser, Moonsie thought dejectedly.

I'm too old to be bothered with a kitten, Angel thought selfishly.

Moonsie and Bandit crept nearer to the carrier to inspect its occupant more closely. The kitten bounced up, front paws on the carrier wall.

"Hey, why won't anyone let me out?"

"It's for your own protection, runt. She doesn't want you to run away," Moonsie retorted.

"As if I'd do that. I like the way this place smells. I like the way *you* smell!" The kitten took a deep breath right down to the tips of its tiny white toes.

Moonsie sighed. Riser's death had all of them feeling older than they were. Did any of them have the interest or inclination to deal with an energetic youngster? The short answer: No.

The older cats retreated to the summer cushions. The kitten stood on its tiny back legs and asked endless questions through the openings in the carrier.

"What kind of bird is that?"

"I didn't like the kibble at my last house. Is this kibble better?"

"What time do we eat?"

"Am I going to sleep there with you?"

"What are the humans like around here?"

Angel got up with an exasperated sniff and stalked out of the garage.

Kittens, she thought. *Too much energy and not enough respect for their elders.*

Moonsie and Bandit soon followed, neither of them caring to answer any of the kitten's questions.

Left behind in his carrier, the kitten drooped.

So much for the "Welcome home!" party, he thought sadly. With a sigh, he curled up in a little black ball and tucked his nose under his tail. Within seconds, he was asleep.

The kitten slept in his carrier for the next few nights. The human let him out during the day to eat and explore. The older cats were conspicuous in their absence, causing the human some concern, but as she saw them coming and going from the old barn for meals, she asked no questions. The kitten, given the name of Chuck, wondered sadly why he was being ostracized. He was used to the company of other cats and began to feel neglected and lonely.

He began to notice a pattern that the older cats followed: they would wait until they thought he was away exploring and then stealthily make their way from the old barn to eat. After his breakfast one morning, Chuck trotted conspicuously out the front of the garage, made a show of heading toward the forest, and then quickly hid in the crotch of a gnarled tree. His duplicity was soon rewarded. One by one, he watched as the cats came up the small rise from the old barn, crossed the road, and in single file, ambled toward the food awaiting them.

Chuck waited until they had disappeared inside the garage and then leaped out of the tree. Quietly, he crept closer to the opening of the garage and then bounced inside.

"*Hey!* Where have you guys *been*? I've missed you! Haven't you missed me?"

Nope, thought Angel and Bandit, heads down in the kibble, much more interested in breakfast than the newcomer.

Moonsie, however, was beginning to feel a little guilty about the way they'd all abandoned the kitten. Would Riser have approved of their neglect? He had given his life for his family. The least they could do was accept this new addition.

He scrutinized the kitten, who, fearing retribution, cowered on the dusty floor of the garage. It looked up. Moonsie looked down. Then he sighed.

"Okay, look. Here's the way it's going to be. We'll come back and stay with you, but there are a few things you need to know."

Chuck brightened immediately. "I'm listening."

"First," Moonsie said, "if any of us are sleeping, don't wake us up. We need sleep even if you don't."

"Got it. What else?"

"Next. Don't climb any huge trees without one of us there to watch you. You could get in trouble and fall down and hurt yourself."

"Okay, okay. Is that it?"

"Out beyond the forest, there are lots of stray cats and other animals. Don't venture out there unless one of us is with you."

And now, I sound just like Riser, Moonsie thought with wry amusement. He glanced at Chuck, who was gazing up at him with something akin to hero worship. Shaking his head, he moved to the cushions and settled down to wash his face. Chuck immediately scampered over and found a spot nearby. He, too, plopped down to wash his face, watching

Moonsie closely for the correct order of operations. Despite his close attention, Chuck's efforts were a complete failure.

Moonsie shook his head. "Did no one teach you how to wash your face properly?"

"There were six of us born at the same time. My mother didn't have time to get into that sort of thing. She was exhausted just feeding us all."

Angel tipped her head, listening to their conversation while feigning disinterest.

Bandit finished eating and joined her brother. Finally, Angel marched stiffly to the cushions and carefully settled herself.

"Come here, youngster," she said to Chuck. "I'll show you how it's done. Proper grooming sets off your fur to best advantage. I know you wouldn't think so now, but when I was a young cat, I had the most beautiful..."

Bandit and Moonsie watched in amusement, as Angel showed Chuck how to wash his face and how to check between his toes for any irritant that could impede his movement. When the short lesson was over, Chuck got up from the cushions, with his little poker of a tail standing straight up, and draped himself over Angel's back legs. He was asleep almost immediately, the sound of his kitten purrs strangely comforting. Bandit made a movement as if to shoo him away, but Angel raised a paw to stop her.

"He's all right. He weighs next to nothing, and his warmth feels good on my old legs." She turned her head to inspect the sleeping kitten. "Well, I guess he's ours, huh?"

"It would appear so," Moonsie said. And just like that, there were again four cats on the summer cushions.

As he grew, Chuck found there was much to be learned from Moonsie, who told him stories about Riser and all he had risked for the others. Moonsie also reminded him constantly about Dilly and the lessons to be learned about associating with stray cats, lessons Chuck took very seriously. Angel told him amusing stories about all the humans in the house and how she got her nickname. Bandit told him the story of her amazing squirrel hunt. With every retelling, the squirrel got bigger, her initial capture of him more difficult, and the subsequent chase in the house more acrobatic.

In addition to spending time with the older cats and enjoying the attention of the young humans, Chuck (who was secretly relieved he hadn't been given a nickname) was beginning to learn the area around the house that the cats considered to be theirs. It included the forest, which stretched behind the house, the area near the little barn and the neighbouring trees, and the small pasture around and near the big barn.

One day, Chuck stepped outside onto the deck after enjoying some indoor cuddles with the younger human. Cocking his head, he heard a series of unusual low-pitched hissing noises down in the small pasture. Cautiously, he crossed the road and trotted down the slope to the big barn.

Peering around the corner of the barn, he could see two enormous, dark birds with bright red featherless heads fighting and posturing over something unmoving in the flattened grass. He stretched up on his back legs as high as he could, but he couldn't see what it was that had gotten these strange-looking birds in such a state. His curiosity was growing by the minute.

How can I get up higher so I can see better? he wondered. A quick glance up the side of the barn revealed no ledges or warped boards on which he could sit. He looked over appraisingly at the posts within the fence surrounding the big barn. Some of the posts were quite small and splintered, while others were large enough to… to support a cat on top!

If I can climb up there, he thought delightedly, *I should be able to see what those birds are doing!*

Taking a quick look to make sure the birds were still occupied, Chuck scampered over to the fence. Confidently, he began to scale the tallest post he could see – one of the gate posts that stood considerably taller than the others. In a few seconds, he found himself precariously balanced on top. It wasn't level, and all his concentration was centred on not falling off.

He realized he needed to get down, but a simple leap wasn't going to work – he was too high up. By tiny increments, he wiggled his backside over the edge of the post and began his descent. His foot touched something slippery instead of rough wood, and he began to slip. Scrambling to get back on, he lost his grip altogether and closed his eyes in anticipation of a painful fall. Instead, something sharp snagged the loose skin on the back of his neck, and his fall stopped abruptly. As he hung on the fence, unable to get up and unable to get down, his eyes snapped open in surprise.

Well, this is quite a predicament. Now what do I do?

He was uncomfortable but not in pain. Yet. He considered meowing for the other cats, but then thought better of it. What could they do to get him down? Stand on top of each other and unhook him?

He realized that human help was going to be needed, so he began to meow, quietly at first (after all, this situation was rather embarrassing) and then a great deal louder (those birds just wouldn't shut up and it really was starting to sting.)

The human heard him from the house and came looking for the location of his cries. She finally found Chuck, hung up on the barbed wire. She called for one of the young humans to help her, and she held up Chuck's body weight so no pressure was placed on the scruff of his neck.

The young human sprinted out of the house, examined Chuck where he was caught, and gently lifted him off the barb. He carried

Chuck back to the house, where they examined his wound, bathed it with warm water, poured a fizzy liquid on it that really tingled, and in reward for being such a good patient, gave him some special treats and a warm drink of milk.

Bandit and Moonsie teased him mercilessly for his graceless fall. But surprisingly, Angel was more sympathetic. She helped keep his tiny wound clean, and explained in detail what the huge red-headed birds had been doing.

"But," she told him sternly, "you have to think about the situations you get yourself into. I know you're interested in everything that goes on around here, but you have to be careful. What exactly did you think you were going to do, perched up on that fence post? Fly like a bird?"

Chuck hung his head. She was right, and he knew it.

Angel softened. "Look, let's go for a walk and think about something else." She stretched carefully and headed out behind the house. Chuck followed her dutifully. The afternoon was uncharacteristically still, and the leaves on the trees barely moved. "Here's another lesson for you, youngster. Let's talk about some of the things you can and can't eat when you're hunting. Not everything you catch is tasty, you know." Angel looked up and pointed with one paw.

"Look at the trees. If they're still, it's easier to hear tiny things scurry in the leaves and the grass." To prove her point, she stopped walking and tilted her head to listen. Chuck imitated her, and to his surprise, he could hear the tiniest of tiny feet scurrying under the bent grasses.

Angel tipped her head toward Chuck. Go get it, she mimed.

Chuck cocked his head again and listened. It was very faint, but he could still hear slight movement. His eyes focused on the location of the sound. He gathered his feet underneath him, ready to leap, the tip of his tail twitching. Eyes narrowed, Chuck felt sure he knew exactly where his prey was. Another second…

He pounced and neatly caught the tiny creature in his front paws. In an instant, he bit its neck and it lay still. It was a little mouse-like creature with a long, pointed snout.

Snack time, Chuck thought triumphantly and began crunching on its body. Almost instantly, he spat it out, coughing and gagging.

Angel said dryly, "You should have waited until I told you whether it was edible." She watched in amusement as Chuck wiped at his mouth again and again, trying to dislodge the terrible taste.

"It's a shrew. You can catch them and kill them and take them to the human. But don't eat them. They're beyond disgusting." She snorted with laughter. "And that concludes today's lesson, youngster."

Still chuckling, Angel strolled back to the summer cushions. Chuck followed her, realizing that he still had a great deal to learn. And he definitely needed a drink of water to get that foul taste out of his mouth. Stupid shrews, anyway.

Chuck's initial interest in exploring gradually evolved and deepened into a more serious interest in protecting "the property" as he began to refer to it. After all, hadn't he been brought here to take Riser's place? Riser had given his life to protect the other cats and Chuck was determined to try to live up to his legacy. The older cats' comfort came before his own, and he unfailingly completed his circuits of the property, taking great care to avoid stray cats.

In between his patrols, listening to Angel's stories and lessons, and spending time inside with the young humans, Chuck matured into a large, handsome, velvety black cat. He kept his white patches scrupulously clean, because Angel would box his ears if he didn't.

As the seasons passed, Chuck noticed that Angel began to retell the same stories and reteach the same lessons. At first, he corrected her and told her he already knew all about what she was recounting. She would be affronted and, as emphatically as she could, stalk off to be alone. Later, she would forget what had made her angry and come back. Eventually, Chuck realized he should just let her tell her stories her own way, without his corrections. And so they whiled away the lazy days, lounging on the deck in the sunshine or tucked in their winter home, warm under the heat lamps.

Late one night, after an exceptionally good supper of chicken bones, scraps, and the salty, delicious sauce the human called gravy, Angel tottered stiffly to the winter home. Despite her advancing age, she still appreciated a good meal. She didn't have the energy to undertake a thorough grooming but contented herself with a brief face washing, after first checking to see that Chuck wasn't watching.

Settling herself directly underneath one of the heat lamps, she slowly curled into a ball and tucked her nose under her tail. She drifted almost immediately into sleep.

She didn't often dream but tonight was an exception. Tonight, she dreamed she was a very young cat, slim and sinewy, with shimmering highlights on her fur. In her dream, she ran gracefully through the forest, without aches or pains. She could leap onto fallen tree trunks easily. She could catch a bird mid-flight – she could do anything.

In the distance in a sunshiny clearing, she could see a beautiful tabby cat. He was gesturing to her to come to him. Revelling in her speed and agility, Angel sprinted swiftly to him. It was Riser.

"I've been waiting for you," he said with a smile. "Are you ready?"

Angel nodded. Riser turned and slowly walked toward a stand of tall trees. Angel looked back over her shoulder. Even though she was dreaming in summer, she could see the heated winter home, as Moonsie, Bandit, and Chuck hurried toward it. She wanted to go back to be with them, but something was preventing her from making the return journey. She bade them all a silent goodbye.

Up ahead, Riser was almost at the row of trees. He turned around and beckoned to her. He looked so happy and carefree. She trotted toward him on legs that felt no pain and with a heart free of misgivings.

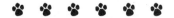

Chuck finished his supper and trotted briskly to the winter home. He had learned his lessons well from Angel and intended to give himself a good grooming before sleep. As soon as he entered the enclosure, however, he could sense that something was amiss. The very air smelled different.

Angel was sleeping underneath the heat lamps. She was stretched out full-length to get the benefit of their warmth. But she was very still. Chuck inched closer and nudged her with his nose.

"Angel?" he whispered. He looked down at her flanks; they were not moving. Then, with more urgency, he cried, "Angel?"

No, no, this can't be happening! he thought in panic. In five strong leaps, he was back with Moonsie and Bandit.

"Something's wrong with Angel! I can't get her to wake up!" Together, the three of them returned to the winter home, Chuck ahead of the older cats. They stopped at its entrance. Moonsie stepped forward slowly and put his head down next to his mother's face. He shook his head sadly and gestured for the other cats to come closer. Together, they lay down next to Angel to keep her company until morning.

At daylight, the human came out of the house with their breakfast and set it down in the garage. She called for the cats briefly, but none of them appeared. She called a little louder with the same result.

She walked toward the winter home and knelt down. The other cats were curled around Angel, keeping vigil over her. She gently displaced them and, more gently still, lifted Angel's body from the enclosure. She pulled the quilt from the cushions and laid the still figure on it. For a long while, the human knelt there, stroking Angel's fur. The other cats stood by helplessly.

The human lifted Angel and placed her in the back of the truck. She returned to the house, and later, the human with the deep voice came out, started the truck, and drove away.

Bandit and Moonsie watched as the truck bore away the body of their mother. Chuck crept in between them, confused and unhappy. The human knew they were unsettled, so she came back out and sat with them. The cats climbed on her lap, one by one, and felt her wordless sympathy.

Much later, the human gently dislodged them and returned to the house, reappearing shortly with a fresh quilt for their winter home. She shook the loose straw off their cushions, patted them back into place, and fluffed the quilt for them. Then patting the quilt, she indicated that they should go back in. It was a little easier then, as the quilt didn't smell like Angel.

Riser's death had been a shock – it had been violent and cruel. But both Bandit and Moonsie understood that their mother was old, that she was in pain, and that the way in which she had died was infinitely preferable to the way in which Riser died. She had had a warm supper and drifted to her forever sleep in the home she knew.

Instead of feeling overwhelming grief at Angel's death, I found myself instead grateful for her long life and its peaceful end. She had given us Moonsie and Bandit, gifts which we appreciated daily. Does it sound ridiculous to say that you learned the manner in which you'd like to leave this world from a cat? Perhaps, but I will say it anyway. And who can ask for more than that?

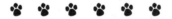

The voices of the young humans woke Chuck from his nap in the forest. He had been dreaming about Angel, and in his dream, they were lazily sunning themselves on the deck, watching the birds at the feeder tree.

He stretched and drew himself to his feet. Where the young humans went, he went too. He padded slowly toward the house and watched as they climbed onto the four-wheeled machine and headed up the road.

Chuck always felt uneasy when the machine bore his young humans away. They went faster than he could keep up, and he didn't like them to be out of his sight for too long. Going at a brisk trot, he set off up the road after them. They were venturing farther than they usually did, and Chuck was alarmed.

They finally stopped at a small ravine, got off the noisy machine, and shut it off. Birdsong harmonized with frog choruses and insect buzzing to complete the early evening symphony. The velvety, elongated heads of the cat tails nodded in the slight breeze.

Chuck finally arrived at the spot where his young humans played. As he sat down, trying not to show just how completely out of breath he was, a slight movement in the long grasses caught his eye. A long, grey-striped tail appeared briefly, twitched, and then vanished. With curiosity and caution combined, Chuck decided to investigate. With a quick glance over his shoulder to check that all was well, he followed a narrow path along the spot where he'd seen the tail disappear.

"Hey, you following me?" The owner of the tail sprang out of the long grass, looking more amused than angry. He had a white face, with grey splotches on his body and dark markings around his ears.

Startled, Chuck stammered, "I... I just wanted to make sure you didn't mean any harm to my humans."

"No evil intentions, my friend. I heard the noise and I was curious to see what it was." He paused before continuing with a mischievous glint in his eyes. "You look like a fine specimen. Up for a fight?"

Chuck was taken aback. First: this presumptuous cat was *not* his friend. Second: it remained to be seen if he had evil intentions. And third: why on earth would he want to fight?

"I have no quarrel with you," Chuck replied stiffly, "as long as you stay away from my humans. And who belongs to you? Or are you... a stray?"

"So what if I am, and who said anything about real fighting? I'm talking about *play* fighting! You must know what it is – it's lots of fun!"

Chuck had never heard of such a thing. Bandit and Moonsie had never mentioned it, and the only "play" fighting he knew was the occasional boxing of the ears he'd received from Angel, only he never really felt she was playing. Distracted by thoughts of Angel, he focused with effort on the cat before him.

"First, we walk around each other in circles," the grey and white cat explained. "Try to look mean. Then I'll grab you around the neck and flip you over. Got it? Then you try it!"

Chuck reluctantly agreed. The two cats circled one another, both trying to look bigger than they were. They raised the hair on their backs and lashed their tails. Then, without warning, Chuck's opponent pounced on him and rolled him over. Then he jumped up immediately and gestured for Chuck to try the same manoeuver. They pounced on each other over and over again.

Chuck was having a marvellous time despite being decidedly out of breath. Why had no one told him about play fighting before?

"So, is there anything else to play fighting other than flipping your partner over?" he asked.

"Oh, yeah – time for the next move. This one is harder, so we'll just see what you're made of. I'll grab you by the throat, throw you down, and use my back legs to kick your belly. And, judging by the looks of yours, it's a big, soft target."

Chuck sniffed in annoyance. "We'll just see about that." They circled one another carefully. Suddenly, his opponent stopped and looked somewhere over Chuck's shoulder. Caught off guard, Chuck turned to see what had caught his eye. Immediately, his opponent sprung; he had Chuck by the throat and was landing surprisingly strong kicks at his soft belly before he even knew what happened.

"Okay, okay – I give up," Chuck whistled, as the air was being squeezed in his throat. The other cat stood up with a smug air of satisfaction. In an instant, Chuck leaped, caught him by the throat, threw him to the ground, and gave him a couple of not-quite-play-fighting kicks in the belly.

His fight partner stood up and looked at Chuck with grudging respect. "Might have underestimated you there, Champ. But I've got one more move to show you." Quick as lightning, he shot out a long front limb and boxed the side of Chuck's face. Three times. Chuck yowled in astonishment.

"I know, right? I've worked hard on that move! I'm a little faster with my left than my right, but I can use them both in a pinch. So, now you know all of it and it's time to put it all together. Neck – flip – throat – kick – slap, slap, slap. Repeat. Got it?"

Chuck repeated the sequence aloud a few times to make sure he had it down. Then, giving the other cat a threatening, hopefully menacing glare, he pounced. And then he promptly forgot everything he had just been taught. His rival pinned him swiftly to the ground by the throat, lightly bit him, and then released him.

"You know, if this was a real fight, I could have hurt you badly."

Chuck got up slowly. His confidence in his new fighting moves was severely shaken. He turned his back on his opponent and, sulking, stalked back to where the young humans were tossing rocks into the ravine and playing in the shallow water. He watched them gloomily. How was he supposed to look after everyone if he couldn't even protect himself in a play fight? He was hugely embarrassed.

"I got whipped in a play fight. Pathetic. I always figured I wasn't much of a fighter, and now I've got proof," he muttered as the young humans climbed back onto the noisy machine.

He pouted as they travelled back down the road. "Great – I risk my life for them, and they ignore me." Still in a huff, he started back down the road by himself, feeling neglected and unappreciated. The young humans soon realized they were without their faithful black guardian and turned around. They picked him up, and he rode back to the house on the lap of the younger human.

Once back at the house, Chuck leaped out of his benefactor's arms and slunk under the deck, head hanging low. The younger human got down on the ground near him and tried to coax him out, but Chuck was having none of it. He was thoroughly disgusted with himself. His gloom persisted until dark, when he walked dejectedly to the summer cushions and flopped down.

Chuck awoke, feeling strangely shivery and cold, even though the morning was very warm. He crept slowly off the summer cushions, shaky and dizzy. Tottering to the deck, he climbed the stairs very carefully and lay down in the warm sun.

Maybe a good sunbath will make me feel better, he thought woozily.

Alarmed, Bandit watched his halting walk to the deck. She followed him and lay down near him. "What's wrong?"

"I'm cold and I can't stop shivering. I ought to be hungry because I haven't eaten since early yesterday, but the thought of eating anything is revolting," Chuck replied through chattering teeth.

Bandit cuddled up very close to him, and draped her chin and chest over his back. She could feel his shivers through her body. They lay that way for a long time until his combined heat from below and the warm sun from above was making her uncomfortable. She lifted herself from his back and settled near him, more than a little concerned. Chuck's shivering hadn't lessened, and he was drooling. He hardly had the strength to lift his head. Hopefully, it was just something rotten he'd eaten and he would soon be better.

Or, she thought apprehensively, *did he get hurt in that senseless play fight?*

For three long days and nights, Chuck remained on the deck with Bandit hovering anxiously nearby. The human was alarmed to see him so lethargic; she brought him tiny soft tidbits and left a water bowl near him. He purred his appreciation for her care and attention.

I'm not much use if I can't look after things around here, Chuck thought miserably. *Maybe I should just walk away and not come back.*

On the morning of the fourth day, Chuck awoke from a restful nap. He got carefully to his feet and realized, to his delight, that he felt a little stronger. The other cats had considerately not eaten the tidbits the human had put out especially for him, and the sight of them made him realize how ravenous he was. He reached out a long limb shakily and dragged the dish closer. Bending his head, he ate one tiny bit of food and then quickly devoured the rest. He heaved a sigh and assessed the damage.

He had gotten thin in those few days, and he could sure use a good grooming. Maybe he could convince Bandit to help him with that task. And it appeared that he might have a drooling issue, which wasn't very dignified.

The human was delighted to see his improved health, and went out of her way to bring him soft food and special treats. As the weeks progressed, Chuck regained the weight he had lost, and to his relief, he also regained his strength and was once again able to resume his daily walks around the property.

The younger human, perhaps feeling partly responsible for abandoning Chuck down at the ravine, often brought him into his bedroom. Then, the younger human would kneel beside Chuck, with his attention focused on a large, square box with a shiny surface.

The box had a long, black string connected to a small, curved object with brightly coloured buttons. The younger human cradled the buttoned object in both hands, pressing the buttons quickly. The buttons appeared to make things happen within the box. There were all sorts of fascinating things happening there: trucks crashed into other trucks, large hairy beasts ate other large hairy beasts, and humans hit balls with sticks or caught ridiculously enormous fish, all accompanied by much noise.

Chuck's favourite position was stretched out right beside the younger human. Together, they would watch what was happening in the box. Occasionally, the human would come in and watch too. She would stretch out on Chuck's other side with her hand on his back, gently ruffling his fur. Apparently, she wasn't very interested in what was happening in the box, as she fell asleep quite often.

The days blended into weeks, and the weeks into months. The young humans grew and were away from the house for longer periods of time. Chuck completed his walks around the property and kept a watchful eye on Bandit and Moonsie during the time the young humans were away, and made sure he was available for indoor time when they came home.

During his rambles late one summer, Chuck occasionally noticed a small ginger-hued tabby lurking near the house. She didn't come close enough to alarm him, but just slipped in to get occasional bits of food and then she vanished. As time passed, he could see that her body shape was changing. He remembered stories Angel had told him about what she looked like before she had given birth to Moonsie and Bandit, and this cat's appearance looked very similar. He suspected that she might try to ingratiate herself into the human's affections.

He couldn't have been more wrong.

CHAPTER SIX

. . . .

GINGEY

The small gingery tabby lay in the long grass behind the house. She was descended from a long line of feral cats who valued their independence and freedom. Yes, she was independent, but she was also practical.

She had seen the human come out of the house and lay down what to her eyes seemed like ridiculously large amounts of food.

No wonder they're all fat as geese, the little tabby thought contemptuously. That thought was proven as the resident cats picked daintily through the feast, ate a few nibbles, and then lounged in their sleeping area.

She crept closer, drawn irresistibly to the food. She was more than capable of hunting for herself, but the new life in her body was making her hungrier than usual. On silent feet, she padded to the scraps and crouched warily down before them. Her need was so great she didn't notice the human watching her through the open window.

In the days that followed, the human left out all manner of tasty tidbits. There were the hard little nuggets and soft mushy food that had a sort of indefinable flavour. But the best part of all? The bits that were human food. The little pregnant tabby developed a taste for all of it.

One day, she watched from only a few yards away as the human set out the morning's offerings. The human didn't appear to see her and vanished into the house immediately afterward. The little tabby trotted directly to the food and ate hungrily. The human watched with satisfaction.

Over the next few weeks, a routine was established. The human would leave a generous helping of breakfast near the porch door, moving it very slightly closer with each meal. And every day, she would leave the door open a fraction of a minute longer. Once she was done feeding, however, the little cat sped away. The human decided to call her Gingey, based on the russet tones in her fur.

As the weeks passed and fall was hinting at the winter ahead, Gingey felt strange twinges in her body. She began to search for a safe and secluded place to nest, sensing that her birthing time wasn't far away. One afternoon, she felt an overwhelming urge to lie down. Panting lightly, she strained and could feel movement in the lower part of her body. She gave a massive push, and a small liquid-filled bag lay in the grass beside her. She tore open the bag and began licking at her kitten's mouth and nose. With each pass of her rough tongue along the kitten's face and body, Gingey felt her love for it intensify. The tiny kitten lifted its head shakily and she nudged it toward her belly.

Minutes later, Gingey felt the same urge as before. Push. Rest. Push. Soon, a second kitten lay beside her. Repeating the procedure, she washed its tiny face and body and settled it near its sibling. Looking with satisfaction at her kittens, Gingey gave a deep sigh of content-ment and curled up around them, keeping them protected from the chill wind.

She woke up near dark, again feeling the same strong urge to push. This time, the process took much longer. She was exhausted by the time the kitten was born. Gingey ripped aside the membrane covering it and began to lick it vigorously. The kitten did not move. More frantically now, she licked its face, its ears, and its tiny body – anything to stimulate it. For a long time, she worked over the motionless kitten. The other kittens gave tiny mews of distress and protest, dislodged as they had been from their mother's warmth and comfort.

Finally, something told her it was of no use. Sorrowfully, she gathered her surviving kittens close. She stretched out on her side to allow the kittens to suckle. Later, with their little bellies full almost to bursting, they cuddled down near each other. Gingey watched them, an undertone of sorrow blending with her joy. As they slept, she felt her head drooping. She curled around them and drifted to sleep.

As they slept, a light snow began to fall.

If it was just me, Gingey often thought over the next few weeks, *I'd find some sort of hollowed-out log or an abandoned building and be quite content there for the winter.* But accommodations that would have sufficed for her alone would not have been an adequate home for her kittens. She left them only briefly to hunt or snatch quickly at some food the human put out. In the short periods of time she was away, she worried about her kittens, who would be shivering with cold when she returned.

There was nothing for it but to rely on the human for help. Early one morning, she carried one kitten at a time to the house and placed it in a large round tub in the open-fronted building where the lazy loungers had their cushions. All she had to do now… wait.

It didn't take long. Later that day, the human rounded the corner on her way to her car and squealed in delight at the two fluffy, round-eyed newcomers peering up at her. Their comfort and support through the winter was assured.

Gingey found there was a fine line to be balanced, once she had placed her kittens partially within the human's care. Yes, she appreciated the shelter that was constructed for her and her babies away from the pampered cats. And yes, she appreciated the cushion, quilt, and heat lamp that were theirs alone. But she was jealous of the amount of time that the human spent with her kittens. They were constantly being fussed over and cuddled.

Who actually gave birth to those things, her or me? Gingey thought resentfully one day. *Those kittens are going to forget where they come from and the proud independent ancestry they have.*

The other cats are no better, she thought scornfully. *All they do is lie in that heated house and wait for meals to be brought to their door. Except the black one. He has a little more ambition.*

As the winter days passed, and her kittens became less physically dependent on her, Gingey's resentment grew. She even went so far as to take her kittens, one at a time, and settle them in a hollow log deep in the forest. But the aggravating things popped out of the log almost as soon as she placed them there and trotted straight back to the house – back to the human and all of the attention and comfort provided there.

There was no one there with whom she could voice her concerns. Moonsie and Bandit had been born there, and Chuck? His only concerns seemed to be spending time inside the house and prowling the area surrounding it. And so, one day in early spring, Gingey turned her back on available food and shelter, and on her own kittens, and vanished.

I had always sensed that Gingey resented the attention we paid to her kittens. Despite our overtures, she had never warmed to any of us. Her departure was not a major surprise, and since her kittens seemed to have been accepted by the other cats, especially Chuck, all was well. The lesson

to be learned in her brief interlude with us was simple: you can't force someone into a change they are not willing or able to make.

The male kitten was a handsome short-haired tabby with dark stripes and white whiskers. My younger son named him Chairman Meow, based on a cat character in a movie he had seen.

His sister had longer hair, similar markings, and an uncanny ability to get into trouble. I lost count of how many times I had to rescue her from precarious situations.

I named her Fluffity, which was a throwback to one of Gram's beloved barn cats, Fluff. And so, thanks to Gingey, Chairman Meow and Fluffity came into our lives.

I only wish their lives had been longer.

CHAPTER SEVEN

· ·

CHAIRMAN MEOW AND FLUFFITY

As spring gradually warmed into summer, Chuck searched for Gingey, not for his own sake but for the sake of the kittens. He even ventured far outside the area of the property but found no trace of her. Soon, it was as if she had never been there. The kittens appeared not to mourn her absence.

Well, Chuck thought resignedly, *if the kittens have accepted their abandonment, then what can I do?*

In an attempt to perhaps make up for the fact that they *had* been abandoned, Chuck took it upon himself to keep an eye out for the kittens. The more outgoing and adventurous of the pair was Fluffity.

The human must have completely run out of imagination when naming her, Chuck thought with amusement. *That was the best she could do?* The other kitten, who was more cautious, had been given a dignified name which Chuck rather liked.

Chuck did his best to impart the important lessons he had learned from Angel, but the two of them were not in the least interested in acquiring any of it, especially Fluffity. When he tried to explain why they needed to invest time in grooming, they gave their faces a cursory wash and darted away. When he tried to show them how to remove a pesky thorn from a paw, Fluffity told him they were too smart to pick up a thorn and ignored him. When he attempted to explain the best way to get down from a tree, she said they were born knowing how to do that.

Arrogant little snips, Chuck thought some days. *I wish their mother was here to deal with them. I haven't got the patience for all of their nonsense.* It seemed to him that all he did for the first year of their lives was to try to find out where they were.

His concerns were valid, as Fluffity especially was showing an alarming tendency to roam far beyond the area Chuck considered safe. One of her favourite things to do was venture out to the road where vehicles passed at far higher speeds than the vehicles in the yard. She also spent considerable time down at the bridge, which alarmed Chuck even more.

One warm early spring afternoon, as Chuck, Bandit, and Moonsie were napping in their deck chairs in the sunshine, Fluffity tried to convince Chairman to go with her down to the bridge.

"Get off those cushions! Jeez, you're going to grow roots," she told her brother, who had been enjoying a quiet afternoon siesta.

Chairman yawned and stretched. "What's the hurry? I'd rather sleep than do whatever lame thing you've got in mind."

"Oh, come *on*," Fluffity coaxed. "I've got an idea for something fun we can do."

Chairman rolled over and re-curled into a ball. "I'm out."

But Fluffity was annoyingly persistent, and realizing he wasn't going to be able to resume his nap until she was satisfied, Chairman stepped off the cushions and stretched. He followed his sister idly down to the bridge and down the incline of the creek bank to the water's edge. Fluffity, in her excitement, had scampered ahead of him and was waiting impatiently.

"So, here's the plan. See all that dead wood in the water?"

Chairman looked at the heaps of grey driftwood wedged against the bridge's support pilings; wind-driven foam decorated its base and the driftwood swayed as the force of the water pushed against it. "Yeah, I see it, but I still don't know where you're going with all of this."

"Look at it! It just about stretches all the way to the other side of the creek bank. I'll bet you I can make my way over to the other side and back again without even getting my feet wet."

Chairman shook his head. "You're out of your mind. Look at all the places you could fall into the water! You don't even know how sturdy some of those old branches are. And what's the point? If you want to get to the other side, just walk over the bridge."

But Fluffity was unconcerned. "I know there's no point. That *is* the point! Do you want to go first?" She gave her brother an arch look, the underlying meaning of which was "Chicken... bok, bok, bok..."

Chairman was torn. On one hand, he was sick of Fluffity teasing him and egging him on to do more adventurous things. On the other hand, and despite the warmth of the afternoon, he had no desire to fall into that water, which was probably deeper than it looked and moving faster than it seemed. With an annoyed grumble, he stepped carefully out on the nearest piece of driftwood. Balancing on it, he bounced tentatively, hoping it would support his weight.

He looked back at Fluffity, who was smirking at him. "Ch- ch- ch- chicken..."

Snapping his head around, he surveyed the pieces of semi-rotted wood, wondering what his next move should be. He leaped onto a gnarled log, which creaked alarmingly.

Enough of this, Chairman thought, and in two bounds, he was back on dry land.

Fluffity looked at him scornfully. "I knew you wouldn't be able to do it. Let *me* show you how it's done." With barely a second to consider where she was going, she leaped out and landed awkwardly on a partially submerged branch. It was slippery and she struggled to maintain her balance. Once she got her feet under her, her confidence returned and she called back over her shoulder, "Nothing to it!"

Chairman called out, "Just forget it! I'll admit you're braver than I am. Satisfied? Just come on back before you get hurt."

"No one's getting hurt. I'll be over and back again before you know it." In half a dozen nimble leaps, Fluffity made her way adroitly to the other creek bank and rolled on the flattened grass in jubilation. Chairman shook his head.

Show-off, he thought.

"Just climb up the creek bank on that side and walk over the bridge. You don't have to cross the logs again. You made your point."

And I intend to make it again, Fluffity thought smugly. Getting to her feet, she picked her way back through the maze of driftwood. Looking to make the return trip more dramatic, she ventured out onto the more slender pieces of wood. Chairman watched in horror as one of the branches snapped, dropping Fluffity into the murky water. Instantly, the current took her downstream.

Chairman raced up the creek bank, under the barbed wire fence, over the road, and down the opposite bank. He could see Fluffity's head bobbing in the water, her feet paddling frantically. "Swim! *Harder!* This way!"

Fluffity's head dipped under the surface of the water. Terrified, Chairman realized she could drown and there was nothing he could do about it. He watched as she was carried farther downstream, resurfacing briefly before the creek rounded a bend and carried her out of sight.

Chairman was immobilized with panic. In anguish, he stared at the bend of the creek around which Fluffity had disappeared. Finally, with no clear plan in place, he sprang up the creek bank and raced back to the house. Chuck was nowhere to be seen. He meowed loudly and pawed frantically at the sliding door, but no one heard his plea. Moonsie and Bandit weren't on the summer cushions. He was almost sobbing now.

Where is everyone?? he thought desperately.

Turning his back on the house, he tore back down to the creek bank where he'd seen Fluffity disappear. He followed the creek downstream, tripping on last year's decayed vegetation, and ignoring the mud and slime on his fur. Finally realizing his mad pursuit was hopeless, he stopped, out of breath and filthy. He collapsed along the water's edge and curled into a ball, heartsick and alone.

Much later, as the sun was beginning to set, Chairman got to his feet. The mud had dried on his fur and something had lodged itself into the pads on one of his front paws. Limping, he trekked slowly back to the house. All three cats were on the cushions as he crept into the garage and collapsed.

Chuck leaped off the cushions. "*What on earth happened to you?*"

Bandit lifted her head, while Moonsie sat up, the better to hear the explanation.

"Fluffity came up with the idea to jump on the driftwood at the bottom of the bridge to get across the creek. She fell in and –" He stopped abruptly and closed his eyes, the image of Fluffity sinking under the water's surface vivid in his mind.

"Where is she now?" Chuck demanded.

"I tried to tell her to swim. I *told* her to swim harder. But the water took her away faster than I could keep up, and I don't know what's –" Chairman hung his head in exhaustion. Bandit examined his fur, and began a careful and sympathetic grooming of his face and ears.

Chuck was struck by an immense stab of guilt. Here he was, lounging on the cushions, enjoying a nap and snacks, while Fluffity was in grave danger. He was supposed to be looking out for them.

Moonsie, sensing his guilt, stepped up quietly beside him and said, "It's not your fault. She wouldn't listen to a thing you said. You can't keep an eye on her every second of the day." He turned to look at Bandit, who was now absorbed in checking out the condition of Chairman's paws. "There's only so much you can do." He repeated, "It's not your fault."

Then why does it feel like it's completely my fault? Chuck thought miserably.

Turning away from the other cats, he padded slowly out of the garage and toward the forest. He stopped abruptly, turned, and trotted swiftly to the bridge and down the creek bank. He easily followed the trail Chairman had made, swerving to avoid the water's edge, the rotting grasses, and the mud. Taking a deep breath, he could smell the place where Chairman had stopped in despair. He looked at the surface of the water.

It's flowing too fast, he thought sadly. *She didn't have a chance.*

He walked slowly back to the garage, a grim and noiseless black shadow. In silence, he climbed onto the cushions where Bandit was completing Chairman's grooming. Moonsie had settled himself on Chairman's other side and moved over to make room for Chuck. Moonsie looked at Chuck and in the darkness, his eyes asked the question: Did you find anything?

Chuck shook his head. Moonsie sighed in disappointment, and after a long time, all four finally slept.

Fluffity tried to open her eyes, but one of them was almost swollen shut. She ached everywhere. Lifting her head carefully, she tried to get her bearings to figure out where she was. She got unsteadily to her feet, coughing violently. The pounding in her head was incessant.

Something must have hit me, she thought dazedly.

"Well, there you are. I was beginning to wonder."

With one eye closed, Fluffity slowly turned her head in the direction of the voice. A slender cat with bright blue eyes, pale fur, and large dark ears was relaxing on the creek bank. Fluffity stared at it in confusion. The blue-eyed stranger stood up gracefully and walked toward Fluffity, who shrank back in fear.

"It's all right. I won't hurt you."

Fluffity sank to the ground, dizzy and nauseated. "What happened? I remember falling off the branches and into the –"

"I don't know anything about that," the blue-eyed cat interrupted. "All I know is you were caught in some bushes at the edge of the creek bank over there." He gestured with a long front limb, his black paw in contrast to his pale fur. "I pulled you out and dragged you up onto the grass. You've been out of it for quite a while."

"Where am I?" she asked. "I don't recognize anything here."

"Well, if you live where I think you do, you're a long way from home. You'd better rest tonight, and I'll help you get home in the morning." The blue-eyed cat hopped nimbly up the creek bank to a sheltered hollow. "Come on up here, if you can make it. Slowly now."

Fluffity climbed carefully up to the hollow. The blue-eyed cat patted the grass, and in gratitude, Fluffity sank down. Its warmth was welcome and she was so, so tired. In seconds, she was asleep.

Her rescuer looked down at her, and then draped himself gently over her back to keep her warm. His eyes closed, and he, too, fell asleep.

Fluffity awoke, aware of warmth beside her that didn't feel familiar. Her eye felt better this morning; she could almost open it fully. She was relieved that she no longer felt dizzy. Her head was still a little sore, but it was bearable. Her companion purred beside her – the sound was comforting.

The blue-eyed cat stirred and stretched languidly. In the morning light, his eyes were bright as jewels. Fluffity stared at him; she had never seen a cat that looked like this one.

"Do you have a name? I mean, a name a human has given you? My human calls me Fluffity. I guess I never thanked you for getting me out of the water."

"You're very welcome." The blue-eyed cat glossed over her question and nudged Fluffity to her feet. "Let's take stock of the damage." He checked her over thoroughly. Her fur was matted and filthy, but she didn't appear to have been seriously injured.

"You could use a good grooming and I imagine you're hungry. The grooming can wait. And if you'll be patient, I'll soon take care of the hungry part."

He sprang up the creek bank and disappeared over the top. Fluffity stood in the little sun-warmed hollow, questions swirling in her head. Where was Chairman? Why hadn't he tried to save her? Anger bubbled up for his neglect and disinterest in her fate. And what about Chuck or Bandit or Moonsie? Weren't they worried about her? Fluffity's hunger drove her anger, and even though she ached all over, she paced restlessly back and forth.

Coming back over the top of the creek bank with a fat field mouse in his jaws, the blue-eyed cat watched Fluffity's agitated pacing.

Ah, he thought, *I think she'll soon be ready to travel.* He leaped lightly down to the hollow and laid the mouse at Fluffity's feet. In four gulps, she crunched it down.

"Thank you," she mumbled, with her mouth full of mouse.

"And again, you're welcome. If you're feeling up to it, let's get you back home." The blue-eyed cat climbed gracefully to the top of the creek bank and gestured for Fluffity to follow him. Slowly, she climbed up, testing muscles that still felt the after-effects of her trip down the rushing creek.

Together, they kept the creek in their sights and weaved their way upstream. With every step, Fluffity found that walking was a little easier, helped by the warmth of the sun overhead. They travelled in silence, until Fluffity realized she hadn't received an answer to her earlier question.

"You didn't tell me if you had a name. A human name."

The blue-eyed cat paused. "I do have a name. It's Tao." He took a few more steps, sighed, and sat down, ostensibly to give Fluffity time to rest but also to tell his story. "I did live with humans, who pampered me every day. I had the choicest tidbits to eat and a bed to sleep in that was all my own. They brushed me and gave me special climbing trees on which I could exercise and sharpen my claws."

"That all sounds amazing. If they looked after you like that, why did you leave?"

"Who said I left? *They* abandoned *me*."

Fluffity was stunned. She had never heard of such a thing. She thought all humans looked after the cats to which they belonged. "But why would they do that?"

Tao looked unseeing into the distance. "Late one night, when we were all sleeping, I could smell something strange. The smell didn't go away, so I got up to investigate. It was smoke, coming from the basement. The smoke got thicker and thicker…"

Fluffity gently prompted him. "Then what happened?"

Tao swallowed hard. "I ran upstairs into the humans' rooms. I jumped on them in their sleep and woke them up. By this time, the smoke had turned into fire, and the fire was eating up everything in its path. The humans couldn't use the stairs or the doors. So, they jumped out of the windows and fell to the ground." Fluffity could tell Tao was struggling to find words to explain how terrified he had been.

"I tried to make my way back down the stairs, but the fire was getting too big. I jumped up to one of the windows and looked out. The fire was consuming the house, and I didn't know how I was going to be able to get out. It was too far for me to jump. Before I could decide what to do, the house collapsed. I fell back into the basement. By this time, other people must have been there to help put out the fire, because I could feel drops of water on my fur. The water eventually poured in and put the fire out."

Fluffity gazed at Tao in sympathy. He continued softly, "They must have thought I died in the fire. They didn't even look for me. I saved their lives and they couldn't be bothered to find out if I was alive or dead. How's that for gratitude? So as soon as I could, I climbed out of the basement and left them. The same way they left me." His anger and bitterness were palpable. "And I've been on my own ever since."

Fluffity sat in shocked silence. She had no idea that humans were capable of such cruelty. Of course, she had heard the stories about Dilly's stray cat friend who had been caught in a human-set trap, but this was different. This behaviour was wanton and cruel. Her warm heart ached for Tao. On his own, deserted by the humans whose lives he saved. It was so unfair.

Quietly, she told him, "If you wanted, you could come and live with us. Our human would take care of you."

Tao shook his head and got unhurriedly to his feet. "I don't trust them anymore. None of them. I'd rather be on my own." He looked at Fluffity directly, his blue eyes intense. "I'm glad you've got humans who care about you and who will be glad to have you back. Not all of us are that lucky. Be grateful."

They resumed their trek along the creek bank, following the bends of the water. The only sound was the soft padding of their feet on the greening grass and the rushing of the water below. As the sun was beginning to drop in the sky, Tao stopped and asked, "Does this look familiar?"

Fluffity looked in the direction he indicated. She could see the bridge in the distance, and under it, the pile of grey and rotting driftwood that had caused her downfall. Now that she had survived, she could see how foolish she had been, and she was beginning to feel guilty, knowing she would have caused so much worry to the other cats and to the human. She nodded.

"I'll leave you here, then. You can make it back the rest of the way. Good luck to you."

"Wait! Are you sure you don't want to be with us?" Fluffity pleaded. Tao shook his head.

"I thank you for the offer, but no. I'll be fine." Tao gazed at her with his bright blue eyes. He turned and Fluffity watched regretfully as he sprinted swiftly away. Before he rounded the bend that would take him out of view, he stopped and raised a paw in farewell. She never saw him again.

Chuck wasn't sure he believed Fluffity's story. It sounded too fabricated. None of the cats he had ever known had bright blue eyes. And to think a stray cat had saved her life? Unheard of.

He was relieved she had survived her ordeal and made it back safely. His relief, however, was counterbalanced by other fears. He was becoming more concerned for Bandit, as her vision was failing rapidly. She was still able to slowly navigate to and from the summer cushions, and the well-worn paths directly around the house – areas she was intimately familiar with.

He was also uneasy about his own health. There were days when chills and shivering kept him immobile on the cushions or on the deck in the blazing sun. He had little appetite and was becoming a shadow of his former self. Instead of making the rounds of the property every morning, he only had the strength to manage once every three or four days. In alarm, the human checked on him constantly and made sure he had the softest of nutritious tidbits to eat and fresh water at hand.

Chairman became his constant companion. In distress, Chairman watched Chuck's strength fade. He who had always been so vigilant about patrolling the property now barely had the energy to hold up his head. As the days passed, Chuck told Chairman more stories about the cats who had lived before him. He sent Chairman out on short rounds of the property, a responsibility that used to be his.

One late fall afternoon, Chuck and Chairman were cuddled together in the sunshine on the deck. Chuck turned his head and looked at Chairman in satisfaction. He had grown into an intelligent, reliable cat, more sure of his own abilities. He nudged Chairman, who was snoring gently.

"Hey, wake up. It's a nice afternoon. Let's go for a walk."

Chairman was delighted to see that Chuck was feeling more like his old self. With his former vigour, Chuck stepped down from the deck and strode out to the forest.

"Are you sure you want to walk?" Chairman asked, concern evident in his voice.

"Absolutely. I feel better today. I want to show you the whole of the property so on days when I'm not feeling quite like myself, you can do the rounds." They walked through the forest, past the small barn, over to the far row of trees, around the bins, and into the small pasture. Chairman couldn't believe how much energy Chuck had. He was stepping lightly with his old grace, and his head was held high. They stopped for a drink at the edge of the creek and sat down for a rest.

Chuck breathed deeply. "This really is a wonderful place to live, you know? I want you to always appreciate it."

Chairman nodded in agreement. "I know. The human is really good to us, and if what Fluffity said is true, not all humans are."

"I've had lots of time to think about what she said about Tao, and I believe her. I don't think all strange cats are a threat, because look at what Tao did for her. He could have left her in that icy water and she would have died. Instead, he saved her life. I'm grateful for that. But there will always be those who pose a danger to you and to those you love. Our job is to try to tell the difference."

Pausing for breath, Chuck gazed down at the slowly moving current of the creek. He looked directly at Chairman and continued, "You're going to have your work cut out for you – keeping an eye on your sister. I don't think almost drowning taught her any lasting lessons."

"And you'll help me, right?" Chairman asked hopefully.

Chuck didn't answer. "Are you ready to head back? The others will be wondering where we are."

Chairman agreed, and they ambled up the creek bank, back to the house and the summer cushions. Chuck climbed on the cushions with a sigh of relief. "Ahhhh, love these cushions." He briefly kneaded the rumpled quilt covering them, pushing it into a more comfortable position. He lay down with his tail wrapped around his feet and settled his head down on his tail. "Join me?"

Chairman climbed carefully onto the cushions, nestling close to Chuck. Their measured breathing and soft purrs rose in gentle waves of sound.

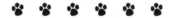

Much later that night, after Moonsie, Bandit, and Fluffity had joined them on the cushions, Chuck awoke. The night was clear and cool, with a light breeze. He rose stiffly and stepped off the cushions, being careful not to disturb the others.

He walked slowly around outside the house, looking for one last time at all the things he had known and loved during his life. He paused, looking up at the window where the younger human had slept and at the deck where the human had sat with him in his illness.

He remembered the day he had been brought here and how he felt when the older cats accepted him as one of their own. He smiled as he recalled Chairman and Fluffity as tiny kittens, and how protective he had felt toward them. He passed the spot where the winter home had stood and walked slowly toward the small barn.

The starlight guided him toward a place just beyond it. He found a hollowed-out spot in the dried grasses and lay down with a sigh.

Yes, I've been a lucky cat, he thought in satisfaction, before he peacefully drifted into the sleep that has no waking.

Breaking the news to the boys that Chuck had died was very difficult. Although neither of them was living here, they mourned his loss along with me. Chuck had been a fixture of their childhoods, a faithful black shadow to them both.

Even though I had been concerned about bringing him here so soon after Riser's death, it was the right decision. He was affectionate, loyal, and gentle. His arrival taught me about the value of acceptance and tolerance. On a lighter note, his escapade with the barbed wire fence showed us all that you should never be afraid to ask for help when you need it!

The surviving cats had difficulty adjusting to Chuck's absence. That winter seemed colder, and even though there was ample space and heat in the winter home, they felt chilled and alone. The human sensed their unhappiness and spent a great deal of time with them outside. She brought them their meals, made sure their heat lamps were working, and turned their cushions and quilts regularly. The attention paid to their physical needs was appreciated, but they sorely missed their faithful black guardian.

Winter refused to relinquish its grip, and it was well into calendar spring before the snow started to melt in earnest. As a result, the winter home stayed in place longer than it usually did. The cats appreciated its warmth and comfort. Even though the days lengthened and the sun tracked a higher path in the sky, the winds blew icy cold, and the cats stayed close to home. Except for Chairman. Chuck had entrusted him with the safety of the other cats and the security of the property. He undertook this venture with such intensity he would sometimes circle the property three different times in one day. He found it hard to relax, and the other cats voiced their concerns.

"You're going to wear yourself out with all your prowling," Bandit told him gently one day. "That's the last thing Chuck would have wanted. I know he asked you to look out for us, but not to the point where you're going to make yourself ill."

Chairman listened without really hearing her. It was his duty to guard them all and he was not going to let Chuck down. Bandit shook her head. She could see there was little she could do, except to let him know they appreciated his efforts.

There was one worrying thing that Chairman hadn't told anyone. During his extensive rounds of the area, he had noticed an increasing number of stray cats. Generally, they were elusive and wary – prone to running as soon as they saw him. But there were the occasional strays who were more aggressive, constantly making their way within the property to their food and helping themselves to the water bowls. It was these strays that kept Chairman awake at night.

Some of the stray cats who lived beyond the perimeter of the property were transient, while others considered themselves semi-permanent: they lived beyond the perimeter but had specific areas in which to hunt and sleep.

One of the semi-permanent strays was a long-bodied, brightly-coloured ginger male. He had remained alive by trusting nothing. He would occasionally venture to the feeding area but sped away at the first appearance of any human. He had learned through bitter experience that humans had ulterior motives and that terrible things could happen if a cat let down his guard.

The first time he ventured inside the perimeter, he used a little-travelled path. Paths of all magnitudes surrounded the property: deer paths, slender paths lightly trampled by mice, and paths used by the cats. He saw that there was food to be had at the house, and he was tired – tired of always having to hunt and tired of constantly having to be vigilant. He was no longer a young cat, and the winters were becoming more of a challenge.

He stepped cautiously out into a clearing and was ferociously broadsided by a snarling, spitting, dark-haired tabby. The unexpected assault rolled him over, and he felt sharp claws digging into his soft belly while the tabby's teeth sank into the loose skin on his neck.

Stunned and pinned, he could only lie there. Chairman let loose his grip long enough to hiss, "Stay off this property. It's mine. If you come around again, I will rip your throat to ribbons." Chairman released him abruptly and stalked away, his tail held aloft in victory.

Still reeling from the events of the last few seconds, the ginger stray picked himself up carefully and checked for injuries. His belly appeared unharmed, but blood was running down his chest from the bite mark on his neck.

That one is sure wound tight, he thought. *I wonder how he would react to someone who was really a threat.*

The days and seasons passed with regularity and routine. Chairman made his rounds of the property, sometimes with Fluffity accompanying him. The older cats kept close to home, for which Chairman was grateful. Bandit's eyesight was almost gone now, and she relied on Moonsie's assistance to guide her from the cushions or the winter home to their meals and back again.

Moonsie, too, was showing the effects of age. His beautiful coat, of which he had been so proud as a young cat, was fading and prone to matting. The one thing Bandit could do for him was help him with his grooming, which she did regularly. The human also brushed his coat, but eventually Moonsie found that the brush hurt his sensitive skin and he shied away from her touch. Something felt wrong inside his body as well; he would eat and eat, and still feel hungry. He became thinner, and soon, even Bandit's gentle grooming hurt his skin.. Without any grooming, his hair matted in uncomfortable clumps along his back. The human tried to remove the clumps with a buzzing tool that cut them off. But Moonsie found their removal more uncomfortable than the clumps themselves.

One bitterly cold winter morning, Bandit and Moonsie slept alone in the winter home. Bandit awoke first, stretching deeply and stepping carefully to a seated position under one of the heat lamps. Moonsie stirred, feeling the absence of her warmth along his side. He opened his eyes, yawned, and sat up beside her.

"What a pair of wrecks we are. Me practically blind and you with your lumpy back," Bandit stated with a wry chuckle. "What happened to the young and beautiful kittens we once were?"

"I have no idea. I can hardly remember what we looked like," Moonsie countered.

Quietly, Bandit said, "I can't even remember what Riser looked like. All I can see is that night when those dogs –"

"Don't. There's no point. It was a long time ago. And I know we've always felt guilty for living when he died. But if we had all died, look how upset the human would have been. If it's any consolation, I can hardly remember what our mother looked like either."

Both of them paused, fixing a fuzzy image of Angel in their minds, and remembering the way in which she had taken Chuck under her care. Looking after one another – that was the important thing. Riser had taken care of them all. Then Chuck had taken on the role. Now,

Chairman was doing the same, although for him, it had become an obsession. The conversation made both cats introspective.

The sound of the human's boots crunching on the snow to bring them breakfast interrupted their musings. The human knelt down with their warmed food, gently stroking Moonsie's head, the only part of him that enjoyed the gesture, and patted the quilts next to Bandit so she would know that she was next in line. Bandit purred loudly and tipped her head back and forth as the human scratched behind her ears, the spot she liked best. Then, both cats settled down to their breakfast. The human watched them, conflicted.

How do you know when it's time? She scrutinized them more closely. Bandit appeared to be in reasonable health, with the exception of her vision, which had gradually worsened over time. Her coat was still shiny and clean, but then, Bandit had always loved to groom not only herself but anyone else who would sit still.

Moonsie was more of a concern. The winters were hard on him, with the clumps on his back leaving bare patches that were more sensitive to the cold. But his eyes were still clear and bright, and he enjoyed his meals more than any other cat she had known.

I'm not ready, the human thought. *I'm never ready when one of them leaves me. But I can't be selfish. I have to think about them over me. Them before me.*

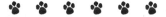

Spring arrived without warning. Almost overnight, the snow melted; tiny rivulets of water ran down the road and the grass began to green.

Warmer weather brought the outdoor cooking smells that all the cats loved. In their garage was a strange device on which the human sometimes cooked. It was a confusing sequence of events: the human would open its lid, stand far back, and toss in a fiery small stick of some magnitude. The device would let out a massive "whoooosh," and fire could be seen in its depths. The human would put down its lid and go back into the house, returning later with meat on a dish.

The cats were drawn to the device, not only because of its good smells but because of its warmth. But there was a fine line: one could sit on the lid for a short time, but if one wasn't careful, burns on one's paws or backside could result.

Returning after a sojourn down at the creek late one morning, Fluffity trotted toward the garage. She had gotten chilled playing in the water, trying to catch some of the annoying tiny fish that lived there. She could smell the cooking device and quickened her pace.

Without first checking with the other cats, Fluffity sailed up onto the lid and landed neatly with all four paws. In the next instant, she leaped off and jumped straight into the water dish.

"Why didn't anybody tell me it was *hot?*" she howled.

On the cushions, the other cats looked on, amusement evident on all three faces.

"You never bothered to ask," Chairman told his sister. "Next time, maybe take half a second to ask before you do something reckless. Not to mention, something that could cause you serious harm. Does this sound familiar at all?" Chuckling and shaking his head, he ambled out of the garage and off into the forest.

Fluffity crawled out of the water dish, refusing to look at or talk to Moonsie and Bandit, and limped awkwardly toward the cushions. She collapsed there and began a minute inspection of the pads of her feet. Red but not blistered. Now that she was out of the cool water, however, her pads began to sting. She was disgusted with herself as well as embarrassed.

Why can't I just think sometimes? she thought, shaking her head. *One of these days, I'm going to get myself into a predicament that really* is *going to be a disaster.*

The next morning, Fluffity found that her feet were still tender. She spent most of the day on the cushions with Bandit and Moonsie, both of whom seemed grateful for her company. She was relieved that, after their initial burst of amusement at her idiotic leap yesterday and her subsequent sulks afterward, neither of them teased her.

Bandit groomed the fur around Fluffity's pads; some had been lightly singed. Her gentle touches eased the stinging and Fluffity thanked her.

"I'm glad to help. It's about the only thing I can do anymore," Bandit said wistfully.

Fluffity looked at her in concern, putting aside for once her youthful and selfish interest in her own well-being. She suddenly realized that Bandit and Moonsie occasionally needed help. And she hadn't been providing it, leaving Chairman to worry about them alone.

"Can I do anything for you? Are you or Moonsie hungry? How about a mouse? I know where there's a nest with a lot of –"

"I'm fine, young one," Bandit said gently. "You don't have to fuss about me. Chairman and the human do enough of that already." Moonsie nodded in agreement. Fluffity looked fondly at both of them – Bandit with her beautiful shiny calico coat and Moonsie with his bright, intelligent eyes. She cuddled in close to Moonsie, and they drifted to sleep.

Long after Fluffity and Moonsie were asleep, Bandit thought about Fluffity's comments.

Am I getting to be a problem? Is everyone worrying about me? That's the last thing I want, she thought in dismay.

Bandit was still deep in thought when she heard the human come into the garage with their supper. She heard the rattle of kibble in its container, and the faint pebbly noise it made when it was piled up in its dish. She smelled their warm supper as it was placed near the cushions, and arched up into the human's touch as her back was gently stroked and the backs of her ears were tickled. She looked up in what she thought was the direction of the human's face and purred in gratitude.

In the morning, the human came out earlier than usual with their breakfast. The younger cats had gone for a morning prowl, and Moonsie looked up as she approached. He was curled up beside Bandit, with his head resting next to hers. The human moved him gently and laid her hand on Bandit's body. It was very still. Again and again, the human stroked the bright calico fur while Moonsie stood by helplessly, feeling lost and alone.

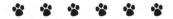

Beautiful Bandit. Beautiful both within and without. Out of the senior cats, she was the one who most appreciated being brushed. Perhaps because she was so engaged in grooming the other cats, having me brush her was the feline equivalent of a spa day. And of all the cats, she was the one who had consistently brought me the spoils of her hunts. Who knew you could learn so much about the importance of generosity from a mangled mouse dropped on your doorstep?

I didn't realize how much I would miss that bright black, white, and orange coat on the cushions until it was no longer there.

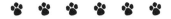

And now I'm the only link to Riser, Moonsie thought in despair. *I'm the only one who remembers what happened to Dilly.*

He remained on the cushions for days, staying close to Bandit's scent and the slight indent left there by her body. The human tried to coax him off the cushions with savoury tidbits especially for him. She stroked his head and spoke softly to him.

Chairman and Fluffity didn't know what to do to help him. They were not of his generation and didn't know how he was feeling at the death of a companion his own age. Fluffity tried to get Moonsie to talk about the old days – when he and Bandit were kittens, or how Riser had rescued him from the tallest tree on the entire property, or about the time when Bandit and the squirrel tore through the house, a story that lived large in all the cats' mythology.

To Moonsie's horror, the human changed the quilt on their summer cushions and fluffed them up, removing Bandit's scent and imprint forever. Perhaps she wanted to help him see a future without his sister, but it was very hard. He ate little, and was listless and unhappy.

Fluffity tried to spend as much time with Moonsie as he would allow. She didn't try to get him to talk, but instead, just sat near him on the cushions, not touching but close by. She brought him small bites of food from the dishes, since he was disinterested in getting up to feed.

Late one night, after Fluffity had cuddled down near him, Moonsie asked plaintively, "Don't you have anything better to do than hang out with an old shell of a cat like me? I'm not exactly great company, you know."

Fluffity chose her words carefully. "I know I'm not Bandit and I know no one can ever replace her. I just wanted you to know that you're not alone. And if you think you don't have anything left to offer, nothing could be further from the truth. I won't say I understand how you feel, because I have Chairman. But you still have both of us. And we need you."

She rose and gently groomed the top of Moonsie's head. His heart ached at the touch of her gentle grooming – a loving task that Bandit used to do for him. It was the final acknowledgement that Bandit was gone, and with it came the realization that she would be appalled at the extent of his mourning. There were still things he could do and care he could give to the younger cats. With an immense effort, he got to his feet and tried to inject some enthusiasm into his voice.

"Thank you, young one. I think I'm going to be all right. How about you bring me a few bites from the dish over there? I believe I'm feeling a little peckish. And if you're out on the prowl a little later, a plump mouse would go down a treat. How about that?"

Fluffity bounced off the cushions in delight, tearing right through the pile of kibble in her hurry to get to the scrap dish. She brought back a tender chunk of baked ham and set it down before Moonsie. "There. Eat that up. And you ordered a plump mouse? How would you like that done, sir? Rare or rare?"

Moonsie chuckled briefly at her antics. "Rare would be fine. Off you go now." He watched her trot from the garage and felt, for the first time in a long while, that he was going to survive. He dropped his head to the food in front of him and gave it a cursory lick.

That's actually pretty good, he thought in surprise and ate it all.

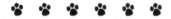

With Fluffity's encouragement, supplemented by Chairman, Moonsie found his interest in life return. He still missed Bandit intensely, but the companionship of the younger cats and the more temperate weather helped a great deal.

Moonsie welcomed the spring sun whole-heartedly. He found it difficult to regulate his body heat, and in the winter home, he was either too hot or too cold. The spring sunshine was the tonic he needed. He spent hours on the deck, warming himself and enjoying the activities of the younger cats.

Fluffity was delighted to see Moonsie's improving spirits. The old cat remained very thin and moved slowly, but he spent less time on the cushions. With Moonsie on the mend, she felt she could leave him for stretches of time to go out on her own adventures. Keeping in mind how devastated he had been when Bandit had died, and remembering how Chairman had felt when she fell into the swiftly rushing creek, she did her best to stay out of real mischief.

Until…

A human-like front paw prodded the summer cushions. Awoken from a light sleep, Fluffity opened one eye.

"Hey, pssssst," a hoarse voice whispered. "You on the cushions. Ya gonna eat that?"

Fluffity was wide awake now. Sitting up erectly in front of the cushions was a plump little raccoon. For many years now, the cats and raccoons had a long-standing agreement: they would ignore one another. And if the raccoons hoovered up a few of the leftover scraps and kibble at the end of the day, they both considered it a win as the human would replenish the supply of both the next day.

The little raccoon leaned in a bit farther and gave Fluffity a poke with its funny-looking front paw. "That pile of stuff over there. Ya eatin' that? And what about the juicy stuff in the cooker? Ya got dibs on that?"

Fluffity looked in the direction the raccoon was pointing. There were six individual bits of kibble and a dried-up piece of roast beef. "Nope. All yours. And why are you even bothering to ask? You lot generally just saunter in here and take it anyway."

The little raccoon stuffed the kibble and the beef into his cheeks. He spoke through his supper. "I'm p'lite."

"What?" Fluffity asked. "Couldn't hear you through all that food in your face." The little raccoon swallowed his mouthful and headed toward the drip tray on the outdoor cooker. Fluffity watched in disgust as his agile paws tipped down the drip tray and sucked back the grease.

"Eeewww, that's *disgusting!* How can you *eat* that?"

Her companion tipped the tray back into place. "For starters, I have no standards."

Fluffity chuckled. "What were you saying before? When you had your mouth stuffed full?"

"I was tryin' to say 'I'm polite.'"

"Well, hi there, Polite. I'm Fluffity," she replied facetiously.

The other cats were awake at this point in their exchange. Moonsie lifted his head from the cushions, and Chairman got directly to his feet. The hair rose on his back, and his ears flattened. He hissed at the intruder.

"*Get out of here*. You got what you came for."

Fluffity spoke up quickly. "It was my fault. I was talking to him."

The little raccoon held up his front paws in surrender. "Not meanin' any harm, Chum. Headin' out now." He glanced at Fluffity. "Thanks for the chat. See ya later." He ambled out of the garage and disappeared into the night.

"It's not Chum. It's Chairman. Chairman Meow to you," Chairman snarled at the raccoon's plump, retreating figure. Then, he rounded on Fluffity. "Are you crazy? Just leave them alone. Don't talk to them. Don't encourage them. Just – just –" Stuttering in his anger and frustration, he finally continued, "Just stay away from them. Sometimes, they get this strange sickness and I don't want you or Moonsie catching it from them."

"He looked perfectly healthy to me," Fluffity retorted.

"He may have been, but that doesn't mean the raccoons he lives with are healthy."

Moonsie nodded in agreement. "Better listen to your brother, young one. He's right. There have been times when the sick raccoons have been near here, and it's nothing you ever want to see. It's just better to keep away from them altogether."

Chairman glared at his sister. He had no time for her foolishness right now. His omnipresent concern for Moonsie and, more pressingly, the one or two stray cats who refused to heed his warnings were occupying all of his time and energy.

Completely out of patience, he hissed at her. Fluffity sank back onto the cushions, confused and hurt. What was his *problem*?

"All right, *all right!* You made your point," Fluffity said sullenly. "I'll leave them alone."

Mollified, Chairman sank back down on the cushions. Moonsie stretched and curled up near him. Soon, both cats were asleep. Fluffity scowled at her brother's sleeping form.

Sure, Fluffity thought, *I'll leave* them *alone. I don't recall I said anything about leaving* him *alone.*

She smiled, thinking about the cheek of that raccoon calling Chairman "Chum." It was amusing, watching her brother being teased. It was good for him, as he did get a little full of himself sometimes in his self-proclaimed role as head of the family and protector of "the property," as he called it. Fluffity remained awake for a long time, wondering if she would ever see their little nocturnal visitor again.

She didn't have long to wait. The next night, she could hear strange noises coming from the direction of the bird-feeder tree. She peeked around the corner of the garage and saw Polite making his way up the tree, branches creaking and bowing under his weight.

What on earth is he after? she wondered. The question was answered as the little raccoon swung down onto a lower branch, inched his way out by distributing his considerable weight on as many branches as he could, and with his deft little paws, snapped open the cage holding the birds' suet block.

In amazement, she watched as the block hit the ground with a thud. Then, with surprising speed for one of his size, he slid out of the tree and grabbed the block with his two front paws. Lifting it to his mouth, he began chomping on the greasy thing.

"And again, eeewww. How can you eat that lardy thing?"

The little raccoon didn't seem surprised to hear Fluffity's voice or see her approaching.

"Full o' protein, ma'am." He held it away from his mouth and offered it to her. "Look at all the nuts in there. This is a good one. Homemade. Full o' seeds too. Want some?"

Fluffity shook her head. "All yours. I prefer my protein in meat form."

"Not adverse to that either. But in my business, ya take what you can get. And you bunch musta been hungry today. Nothin' left over in either the kibble or the scrap department." He returned his attention to the bird block.

In three more huge greasy bites, it was devoured. The raccoon burped gently and used one of his flexible paws to pick at his teeth. "Seeds. Get 'em caught in my back teeth ev'ry time." He burped again. "So, what's shakin' tonight? Where's your guardian?" He drew the last word out, and made it an insult – "gaauurrdiiaann."

"He's doing an evening prowl. There have been some stray cats around here that he's concerned about, so he's been spending more time out there than usual."

"And what about you? What do ya do for fun?"

Fluffity was a little taken aback. "I don't know. Not a lot, now that you mention it. I keep an eye on Moonsie and try to stay out of trouble so my brother doesn't have to give me a hard time."

"Moonsie, the old one? The one with the fur that looks like a turtle shell?" the raccoon asked impertinently.

Fluffity bristled and immediately rose to Moonsie's defence. "Don't you dare talk about him like that! He's been here since I was a kitten. He's my friend."

The raccoon held up a paw in mock surrender. "Sorry. Can see that's a bit of a touchy subject. Won't mention it again." He waddled toward the water dish and took a few long, loud slurps, splashing water on his face. "Tell your human to freshen this thing up in the mornin'. Water's a little stale."

You've got some nerve, Fluffity thought, *coming in here like you own the place and telling me what's wrong with everything and everybody.* She opened her mouth, ready to tell him her opinion of *him.*

The raccoon, sensing his welcome was rapidly wearing out, turned on the charm. "So, y'asked me what my name was the other night and I didn't tell ya. I'm tellin' ya now. It's Digger."

Slightly pacified, Fluffity replied, "I thought only humans gave out names. Did a human give you that name?"

The raccoon rolled his little black eyes and scratched an ear delicately. "No, not everything revolves around the humans, ya know. My mama gave me my name, because I like to dig holes in just about anything. Wanna see?"

He turned his back on Fluffity, and in less time than it takes to tell it, he scampered back to the bird-feeder tree and dug a hole in the grass underneath it into which almost half of his body could fit. He popped up, damp soil on his paws and nose. "Makes sense now, huh? Wait a minute – I think I felt somethin' down there."

He resumed his excavating and emerged shortly after with a small dirt-covered object. Waddling to the water bowl, he swished it back and forth under the water while apparently staring off into space. Fluffity shook her head. *Strange creatures, these raccoons.*

Digger held his prize aloft in victory. "Ta dah! No idea what it is, but here ya go." He tossed it toward Fluffity, and it fell on the grass near her with a soft plop. She prodded it daintily with her paw and rolled it over. It appeared to be one of the little toys Chuck had told her about; the young humans had played with them.

"Wanna see where I live? It's way back out through those trees behind the house, then ya go across the road, and it's down near where the water runs through a little low spot."

Fluffity shook her head. "Chairman wouldn't want me venturing out that far. And if you remember, he doesn't want me having anything to do with you in the first place."

"Awww, come on. Y'r not a baby. Can'tcha make up y'r own mind?" The little raccoon's eyes glittered with challenge. "I dare ya. Don'tcha wanna see how the other half lives?"

Fluffity sat up straighter. This annoying, mouthy grease-licker was daring *her* to do something? She who had almost drowned in the flood of the century? And survived unaided?

Conveniently forgetting Tao's assistance in the heat of the moment, she replied, "Lead on, Digger. If you can make it that far." She looked in disdain at his plump figure.

Digger grinned and gestured with his paw. "This way."

With surprising speed, he rounded the corner of the house and disappeared into the forest. Fluffity bolted after him with some misgivings. Despite her bravado, she knew Chairman would be furious if he knew what she was up to. Pushing those concerns to the back of her mind, she gave herself over to the delight of adventuring late at night to places unknown.

Fluffity stopped in amazement. "You mean *all* of you live here?"

Digger nodded and gestured at the larger raccoon and the five smaller ones who were scattered at various points up and down the ravine. "That's Mama, and my brothers and sisters. We were born here and once we get grown enough, we'll go out on our own. I'm gonna move a long way away from here, but," he gestured with disgust at the two smallest raccoons, "those two are big babies and they'll likely find somewhere to live close to Mama." As if to prove his point, the two smallest raccoons scampered closer to their mother.

Fluffity crouched down and peered into the hollow log that was their den. It rested in a sheltered area of the ravine and looked quite cozy.

"Did you hollow this out all by yourselves? That looks like a lot of work!"

"Nah," Digger replied. "That *would* be too much work. It was already hollow when Mama took it over. Not sure who lived in there before us. Mama just added some leaves and dried grass and twigs to make it homier."

"I can't imagine that's very comfortable to sleep on. But then again, you have a lot more padding than me," Fluffity chuckled.

Digger agreed. "True. Show me a skinny raccoon and I'll show ya a sick raccoon."

Suddenly, Chairman's and Moonsie's comments came back to her – their remarks about sickness in raccoons and how it could be passed to other animals. She backed up from the den quickly and said, "I'd better get back. They'll be wondering where I am." She glanced around surreptitiously, trying to get her bearings.

"Ya know how to get back home?" Digger asked. "I kinda brought ya here by the scenic route."

"Of course I do. I'll be fine." She started off confidently but was interrupted by Digger after she had taken less than two dozen steps.

"Ah, wrong way there." He pointed out the correct direction with his slender paw, his little black eyes gleaming with amusement.

"I knew that!" Fluffity bluffed. "I was just checking out what was happening over there, with your... ah, with your..."

"That would be the loo," Digger chuckled. Behind her, Fluffity could hear the other raccoons tittering with glee.

Fluffity blustered, "And a lovely one it is, too. Well, I'll be off now." She scampered away quickly before she could embarrass herself any further.

Digger watched her go. *Cats,* he thought, shaking his head. *Strange creatures.*

On her way back home, Fluffity replayed the entire embarrassing episode in her head.

Is there any possible way I could have humiliated myself further? she thought with chagrin. *I mean, seriously, I would have to have zero sense of smell not to realize I just about stepped in their* business. *How disgusting would* that *have been!*

She stopped and chuckled, and said aloud, "Especially knowing what they eat!"

Still thinking about the raccoon den and the plump mother and her identical babies, who looked so different from kittens, she trotted up the ditch and stepped out into the road. She was so engrossed in her thoughts about the raccoons in general and about Digger in particular that she forgot where she was. She forgot the rules that had been drilled into her since kittenhood about crossing roads. She turned in time to see blazing lights racing toward her and was immobilized with fear. She never knew it when her body was flung into the ditch, battered and bloodied, and far from home.

Moonsie awoke from a restless sleep. He was alone on the cushions, a state of affairs he did not appreciate. Standing up unsteadily, he stepped carefully off the cushions and walked to the entrance of the garage. There was no sign of either of the younger cats. But he could smell that a raccoon had been there recently.

Once out in front of the house, he could see that the water dish had been muddied and there was a fresh hole dug in the grass near the bird-feeder tree. Bending down stiffly to sniff it, he could tell that a raccoon had dug it. Nearby, he found some fragments of the suet block, the opened cage rattling loudly in the strong breeze above him.

Feeling more and more uneasy, he walked back to the cushions and lay down, staring unseeingly out the garage entrance.

Where are they? he thought with increasing alarm. *They should be back by now. What will happen to me if something happens to them?*

It was dawn before Chairman arrived home after his night patrol. The stray cats were getting bolder, and it was becoming more difficult to keep them away from the property. He was still preoccupied with thoughts of the intruders when Moonsie's voice brought him back.

"It's Fluffity. I don't know where she is. She left when I was sleeping and she hasn't come back. There was a raccoon here and I wonder if –"

"If that mouthy raccoon talked her into going off on some wild adventure," Chairman said. "I wouldn't be surprised. She'll come wandering back in here with some ridiculous story about how she –"

"I don't think so. She'd be back by now if that was the case."

Chairman looked at Moonsie with dismay, the older cat's fear now transmitting itself to him. "I'll go looking for her after breakfast," he said. "Don't you go out – it'll be too much for you."

Moonsie nodded reluctantly. The porch door opened and the human brought their breakfast into the garage. He stared at it without appetite. The human bent down and gently stroked his head, but Moonsie didn't purr in appreciation. His concern was becoming all-consuming.

The porch door opened again; the human with the deep voice climbed into his truck and drove out of the yard. Chairman heard the engine noise fade into the early morning mist. He stepped to the breakfast dish and hunkered down before it as Moonsie watched impatiently from the cushions.

First, those strays and now Fluffity, Chairman thought in frustration; his breakfast tasted like sawdust. *She promised me she wouldn't get into trouble. Why can't she just* listen?

A little later, the truck's distinctive sound could be heard coming back to the yard. The human with the deep voice got out of the truck, leaving the door open, and went quickly into the house.

Chairman sensed what Moonsie already knew. "Jump up in the back of the truck and see…" He couldn't finish the sentence.

Chairman walked unsteadily toward the truck and leaped lightly onto its open tailgate. Lying inside, he could see the body of his sister, her beautiful coat bloodied and torn. The sight was sickening.

He dropped out of the truck and crept back to Moonsie. They huddled on the cushions in grief and shock. Inside the house, they could hear the human crying.

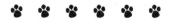

Less than two years. That's how long Fluffity was with us. The death of a young cat is as shattering as the passing of a cat who has been with you for close to two decades. I know I can't control where they go and what they do, but I wish I had some way to minimize the hazards.

From the time she was a tiny kitten, Fluffity had been a risk-taker. I am not – I never have been. I know there have been situations in my own life where I should have taken a chance - thrown my hat over the fence, as the old adage states. I am unlikely to become an impulsive, adventurous, free spirit at this stage of my life, but this I know for sure: sometimes, I wish I could have been.

For a long time after Fluffity's death, Chairman blamed himself, even though he knew he was not directly responsible. Fluffity was fully grown, even though her actions proved otherwise. Her inability to perceive danger infuriated him. Her death meant he had not only lost a littermate, he had – even though they had often been at odds – lost a friend.

Between his grief over Fluffity and his increased patrolling of the property, keeping both stray cats and now raccoons at bay, Chairman was wearing himself out. Moonsie, between his sorrow over Fluffity and his concern for Chairman, was feeling the strain too.

One morning, he tried to voice his concerns as gently as possible. "I know you're hurting, but you're only going to make yourself sick. You're not sleeping. You're barely eating. You have to take care of yourself."

Chairman, thin, exhausted, and dejected, finally nodded. "I know. I'm so tired I can barely put one paw in front of the other, and nothing the human brings us interests me. I know I have to let it go, but it's so —"

"Difficult," Moonsie said softly. "You remember how hard it was for me after Bandit died. I understand. I wanted to leave and never come back. But you and Fluffity made me see that it was still worth being here. Being present... and being a friend."

Chairman could hardly keep his eyes open as Moonsie's soothing voice rolled over him in a warm and comforting wave. "It wasn't your fault. None of it was your fault. Just go to sleep. Just let it all go..."

Chairman's eyes drifted shut, and soon, he was deep in sleep. Moonsie lay awake beside him, feeling his age in every fibre of his being.

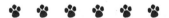

As the weeks passed, Chairman began to feel more like himself. He enjoyed the extra tidbits the human put out for them; eventually, his coat regained its gloss and sheen, and his interest in the things around him returned. He still had occasional days when his sadness resurfaced, but by the return of winter, those days became rarer.

Winter passed quietly, with Chairman spending less time away from the winter home out of consideration for Moonsie. In his turn, Moonsie was comforted by the younger cat's company and by the company of the human, who came out to the winter home often to sit with them.

On the afternoon that the winter home was taken down, Chairman and Moonsie sat nearby, supervising the process. Their heat lamps were stored in the garage, their winter cushions wrapped to protect them from insects and bird droppings, and their winter quilt replaced with a summer one.

"Well, we made it through another one," Moonsie said quietly.

"We did," Chairman replied. "Will you be all right if I go for a quick prowl?" With the return of milder weather, Chairman had again noticed the appearance and traces of many stray cats. While he didn't begrudge the extra time he had spent over the winter with his old friend, he felt he had been neglecting his duty.

"You go on, young one. I'll be fine. There's a patch of sunshine up on the deck that has my name on it." He smiled fondly at Chairman. "Go on."

"All right, but I'll be back as soon as I can." Chairman turned and trotted off across the road. Moonsie watched him disappear over the creek bank and then carefully stepped up onto the deck. With a sigh of relief, he lay down in the warm spring sunshine. Despite his protestations of good spirits and reasonable health, he was not being honest with Chairman. He was not being honest with himself.

He stretched out onto his side to absorb as much sunshine as he could and slipped into a light sleep. He was awakened shortly by a piercing, unfamiliar meow. A small brightly-coloured calico cat was sitting under the bird-feeder tree. Moonsie blinked rapidly. Was he dreaming or was he awake? He got to his feet, and realized he was indeed awake.

He kept his eyes on the little calico cat as he climbed down from the deck and padded toward the bird-feeder tree. He looked down to avoid stepping in a small hole dug by one of the raccoons, and when he looked up, she was gone.

Moonsie swung his head around wildly. Where did she go? Suddenly, it became imperative that he find that little calico cat. He could see a flash of black, orange, and white in the forest. With an almost gravitational pull, he followed the flashes of colour. Just as soon as he reached them, they disappeared again.

Moonsie was exhausted and discouraged. *What am I doing? I know Bandit is dead. Why am I following this mirage?* he thought, shaking his head in dismay and confusion. He was too far from home and Chairman would be worried. He turned slowly to begin the trek back and saw again the shape of the little calico cat. He kept his eyes on her as he walked unsteadily forward. The image stayed in place. As he got closer, he noticed the markings on her face. Beautiful black markings across her eyes.

"I found you, I found you," Moonsie murmured. "Don't leave me."

"I won't," the image replied gently; her beautiful, unclouded eyes gazed at him with deep affection. "I'm here with you now. You're safe. Close your eyes. Rest."

With gratitude and an overwhelming feeling of happiness, Moonsie closed his eyes for the last time.

Chairman returned home from his patrol and found the cushions deserted. Moonsie sometimes took very short sojourns into the forest or across the road into the small pasture, but he was never gone for long. But when night fell and he hadn't returned, Chairman became alarmed. What if Moonsie couldn't hear a vehicle coming? What if a coyote got him? His imagination conjured all sorts of dire possibilities.

When daylight came, Chairman was still alone. Alone on the cushions, with a heavy weight in his heart, he knew that Moonsie was gone.

For the first time, Chairman neglected his patrols.

What's the point? he thought dispassionately. *Who cares? There's no one here for me to protect. I don't care about any of it anymore. I don't even care about myself.*

Gentle Moonsie. He had never caused a minute's trouble, as he preferred home to any other place. But his passing marked the end of an era. Angel, Chuck, Bandit, and Moonsie had grown with my boys. I missed the young cats they had been and, at the same time, found myself missing the children my boys had been.

I had taken a picture of Moonsie with my first digital camera – in the photo, he is lying with stately dignity in front of the garage, his beautiful grey-striped coat in immaculate condition. That photo is on a bulletin board where I can look at it every day. His life was a reminder that it doesn't matter where home is. If those you love are there, that *is home.*

Now all alone, Chairman, too, stayed close to home, which was uncharacteristic behaviour for him. I felt sure, despite his usual independence, that he was lonely. I wanted to bring home some new additions, both for his sake and mine, but hopefully without the initial conflict that had resulted from Chuck's arrival. A friend's cat had had a large litter, and new homes for some of the kittens were in order. I brought home two beautiful, silky, grey and white kittens.

And so Smokey and Misty came into our lives.

CHAPTER EIGHT

· ·

SMOKEY AND MISTY

Returning one day in late summer from a nap in the forest, Chairman turned the corner into the garage and stopped short, almost as if someone had glued his paws to the concrete. His eyes narrowed, a growl emanated from deep in his chest, and the hair rose on his back. Staring back at him were two small puffs of grey and white. One had a bright pink nose and ridiculous markings on its face that made it look rather witless. The other one had more symmetrical facial markings, but it looked as if it had run full-tilt into a wall.

Well, the human certainly didn't pick them for their looks, Chairman thought wryly. The smallest grey bit scampered toward him, ignoring all of the warning signs to stay away. Chairman swatted it with enough force to roll it over, just to let it know who was in charge around here.

The swat did nothing to deter it, and it bounced upright.

"Hi, the human is going to call me Misty. I just love it here. Look at all those birds. Have you seen any squirrels? I love squirrels. How long have you been around here? Are there any other –"

"Would you just take a breath?" Chairman raised a paw to slow her down. "Jeez, you just got here and you're talking my ear off already." He sighed. "I can't take a lot of that inane rambling." He shifted his gaze to peruse the second kitten. "Are you going to introduce me to your friend?"

Misty brightened immediately and scooted back to the other kitten, trying without success to push him forward. "This is my brother, and the human is going to call him Smokey. Don't you think that's a good name? What's your name? Will we sleep with you? I like sleeping with lots of other —"

"Why don't you let your brother get a word in?" Chairman said, shaking his head in disgust. He narrowed his eyes at the silent kitten, who seemed to be sinking lower into the dusty concrete floor with every passing second. *Great first impression,* he thought. *This one is scared of his own shadow.* "What do you have to say for yourself?" he asked.

As Chairman ambled toward the summer cushions for a leisurely grooming, Smokey stood up shakily. His fur was coated in dust, bits of dry leaves, and dead bugs. "I didn't want to come here. I liked it where we were. I don't know why we had to leave."

I don't want you here particularly either, Chairman thought ungraciously. He took a second look at the shivering kitten, gazed into its eyes, and then realized there was something behind its rather witless expression. He spoke more harshly than he intended.

"The human wanted more cats because I was the only one left. She loves them, and if you're here, you've got a good thing going on. Appreciate it, because she's the one who belongs to us. Not to any of the stray cats around here. Us."

Smokey nodded and shot a glance at his sister. She was staring at Chairman with wide eyes.

Chairman continued, "And if you're staying, there are a few things we need to get straight right now. Come with me." He rose and gestured with his paw.

To his immense surprise, Smokey trotted toward him and looked up at him trustingly. Chairman waited for Misty to join them. She was busily engaged in playing with some stray threads on the summer quilt.

"You! *Now!* Let's go!" he snapped. Misty released the threads reluctantly and padded over beside her brother. Chairman rolled his eyes, keeping a tight grip on his temper.

"Lesson number one: I'm going to show you where it's safe to explore. Pay attention to what I'm going to say as if your life depended on it. Because some day, it might."

Wide-eyed, the two kittens followed Chairman as he trotted out of the garage and around the corner. "This," he gestured widely at the four rows of trees behind the house, "is the forest. It's safe. You can wander through it as much as you like." He pointed toward a small red building through some tall trees. "And you can go over there. It's safe too." He turned abruptly and pointed across the road. "You can also walk across the road and explore the pasture. But," he stopped and scowled at the kittens, "you need to always, *always*, stop and listen and look for anything that's coming down the road. Only then, after you know it's safe, do you cross the road." He looked down at the kittens. "Understand?"

Smokey nodded, looking back over his shoulder at the forest and at the small red barn. He raised himself up on his back legs to peer across the road. Chairman turned to Misty, who was energetically chomping on a grasshopper she'd just caught.

"Were you paying the *slightest* bit of attention?" he asked in annoyance.

"Forest, small red building, road. Check it first. Got it," she replied pertly.

Chairman narrowed his eyes. *Kittens,* he thought, with a sudden and full understanding of how he and Fluffity had aggravated Chuck with their antics and refusal to listen. He chuckled, his spirits lifting slightly.

"That'll do for today. I have things to do. You two get back to the cushions and stay there until I get back."

Smokey nodded immediately and trotted back toward the garage. "You too!" Chairman hinted broadly, looking at Misty. Having finished her grasshopper, she bounced up and swiftly caught up to her brother, rolling him over on the grass before they both rounded the corner of the garage.

One warm fall afternoon soon after their arrival, Misty was playing in the bird-feeder tree, trying to catch an unwary sparrow. She had her eye on one particularly fat sparrow that appeared to be dozing near the top of the tree. Misty crept along one branch, waited for a little while, then moved by whisker-widths upward. *Be patient,* she warned herself. *Just take it slowly.* She stepped out on a very narrow branch, which creaked alarmingly. The sparrow opened its eyes briefly, took a desultory look around, then fluffed its feathers and sank back into its nap.

Almost there, Misty thought. *Just a little farther...*

A magpie landed under the tree, looking for bits that had fallen from the suet cage. It squawked loudly with satisfaction. At the same moment Misty reached for the sparrow, the narrow branch she was balancing on snapped. She fell awkwardly to the ground, twisting one of her back paws as she landed.

Smokey was watching her from his vantage point on the deck. "So much for cats being able to land on their feet," he jeered.

"Oh, stuff it!" Misty snapped. "At least, I'm out there trying to earn my keep. All you do is lie there. You're beyond useless!" She attempted to walk away as if nothing had happened but found to her chagrin that she could not. She limped slowly to the cushions in the garage and inspected her foot. It was swelling rapidly and even giving it a tentative lick was painful. Both her pride and her foot ached.

Smokey rounded the corner of the garage. "So now what, Graceful?"

Misty bit back a smart retort. "Go up to the big window and call for the human. If she hears you there, she'll come out to see you. And then you can bring her in here."

Smokey did as he was asked, and shortly, the human was on her knees beside the summer cushions, examining Misty's badly swollen foot with alarm. She disappeared inside the house, returning shortly with a small towel. She spread the towel inside the carrier that had brought them to their new home, gently coaxed Misty inside, and snapped the door closed. Smokey was alarmed to be excluded from these proceedings and followed the human anxiously as the carrier was deposited on the front seat of the car.

Smokey watched in despair as the car rounded the bend and disappeared from sight. He felt completely alone. Was Misty coming back? And where was Chairman? *And who is going to feed me my supper?*

Sometimes, Chairman liked to take his naps out behind the house. It was cool there in the long grass and the treetops whispered to him as he slept. And to be honest, he liked a little alone time away from Misty and Smokey. Training them up *was* rather exhausting. Smokey had the potential to be an effective guardian cat, but that mouthy one couldn't sit still long enough to learn anything.

I'll do my best, he thought, *but I'll bet she's going to get herself into trouble.* Chairman stretched lazily and listened to the insects buzzing in the bushes.

His peaceful idyll was interrupted by the sound of someone frantically charging through the grass as though pursued. Chairman leaped to his feet, ready to defend himself and the property. Smokey burst into Chairman's space, breathless and panicked.

"She's gone! The human took Misty somewhere in the car because her foot was hurt from being in the tree and she fell and I don't know where they —"

"Take a breath and explain it to me again." Chairman sat down, trying to make sense of what had happened. "The human took Misty in the car and...?" he prompted.

Smokey took a huge breath. "She was in the bird-feeder tree and fell out of it. She hurt her foot, and it was really big and she said it hurt, and I don't know what..."

Chairman closed his eyes. Getting information out of this one in a crisis situation was a challenge.

"Let me explain something to you. If Misty hurt her foot, and the human took her away in the car, I would think that Misty is going to the vet."

"What's a vet?" Smokey asked, his breathing beginning to return to normal.

"A vet is a person who looks after animals when they are hurt or sick. Or sometimes, animals are taken there when the human wants to make sure they don't have any babies." Chairman looked at Smokey closely to see if he understood the implication of *that* statement, but there was no change of expression on the younger cat's face.

He hid a small smile. "Sometimes, after you come back from the vet, there are small bits of funny-tasting stuff that the human makes you eat. The small bits that you eat will help make you better. The vet will look at Misty, and then the human will bring her home. It's all going to be fine."

Smokey looked at Chairman with wide eyes. "How do you *know* all of this? Who told you? Have you been to the vet before?"

Chairman nodded. "I have. And see? I'm just fine. She'll be home before you know it." Chairman turned to walk back toward the house and gestured for Smokey to follow him.

From deep in the forest, a large, coal-black cat heard every word. He shifted his position slightly to watch the two cats disappear around the corner of the garage before he rose and padded silently away.

In the car, Misty couldn't get comfortable. She hobbled around inside the carrier, trying to find a way to lay down that didn't put pressure on her foot. The human spoke calmly and soothingly to her. But the idle chat didn't help. Misty's anxiety rose.

Her fears were amplified as the car stopped and she was carried up steps into a building that smelled strongly of other cats and dogs, as well as some sort of pungent aroma she couldn't identify. The human lifted her gently out of the carrier and showed her foot to a stranger, who pulled on it and twisted it and squeezed it. Misty yowled in pain, and the stranger let her foot go.

The human cuddled her briefly, and Misty was so relieved to be away from the pain-causing stranger that she showed her appreciation by cuddling closer still. She could sense the human's complete amazement at the gesture, and thought, *Yeah, don't get used to it. You're just the better choice right now.*

The human placed Misty back in the carrier, and she and the pain-causer spoke briefly. Left to her own devices, Misty looked around at the strange room.

There were countless different smells, and enormous multi-coloured bags of kibble were stacked in piles of varying height. From somewhere outside the room, Misty could hear the muffled and constant yapping of an apparently brainless dog. Looking out the back of the carrier, she could see a huge tabby sleeping on a hair-covered chair.

Inside cat, Misty thought disdainfully, *pampered and lazy.*

As though the tabby sensed he was being scrutinized, he opened his eyes and laboriously jumped down from the chair. Misty shrank back in her carrier as he approached its door.

"Hey, what happened to you?" the tabby asked in a deep, gravelly voice. His stomach drooped almost to the floor, his fur really needed grooming, and his eyes had dark brown spots in them.

"Hurt my foot falling out of a tree," Misty answered in relief. "My own fault. I was trying to catch this sparrow and —"

"Not concerned about the details," the elderly tabby said dryly. "Just wondered if you were staying. But if you're back in your carrier, you're leaving soon." He turned slowly and headed to his chair.

"Wait!" Misty called after his retreating figure. "Where am I? And who are you?"

"You're at the vet clinic. This is where hurt and sick animals come. I live here. I've lived here all my life. I visit with the animals that stay here, I lounge on that chair over there and at this stage of my life, I just tell the mice to get lost. Can't be bothered to chase them anymore." The tabby yawned widely, showing the pink and speckled inside of his mouth. "You're lucky. Your human cares about you or she wouldn't have brought you here."

Yeah, right, Misty thought. *I thought that stranger was going to pull my foot clean off.* Any further speculation was cut short, as the human picked up the carrier and went down the steps and back into the car.

Once home again, Misty looked around her with satisfaction. The carrier had been put away, and the human had brought her a tasty snack to compensate for the uproar. Her foot still ached, but if she was very careful, she could place a little weight on it. Smokey had told her about the funny-tasting bits she might have to eat, but there was no evidence of them yet.

The next morning, however, the human picked her up off the cushions and carried her into the house. She set Misty down on a blanket and held her gently as the human with the deep voice stuck two funny-tasting bits way back in her throat with a long stick. The bits were tiny and went down easily. She sensed their satisfaction with both their efforts and her ability to cooperate.

The same routine followed for the next few mornings: pick up, set down, bits in, back out. Misty found that there was little reason to complain about it, as the human with the deep voice was gentle and the little bits didn't hurt her throat. Her foot improved rapidly and the only lasting effect of her accident was one misshapen back toe.

The first winter storm of the year arrived early. The howling northwest wind rattled the elms' branches overhead with vicious force. Limbs snapped off and crashed onto the hard ground, some splintering into smaller pieces. Inside their winter home, Chairman, Misty, and Smokey shifted restlessly. The wind was keeping them awake and they were chilly, despite the glow of the heat lamps above them.

"Shove over," Chairman growled. Conveniently forgetting about the "equality under the lamps" rule that had existed when he was a kitten, he felt he deserved seniority in terms of the best placement. Chairman kneaded his paws roughly into Smokey's soft stomach, and with an air of resignation, the young cat rose and settled himself near the back of the winter home. Misty followed and cuddled down beside Smokey.

"Why does he always hog the heat? It's not fair. We live here too," Misty whispered. "I like it better when he's not here."

"Shhhh," Smokey cautioned quietly. "Be careful what you wish for. Granted, he can be a royal pain in the paws some days, but he looks out for us. Don't you remember when he told us about that ginger stray who was hanging around? Who knows how many other threats are out there? He keeps us safe."

Misty huffed and, in one smooth motion, draped herself over Smokey to combine their heat. "Maybe, but I still don't like being pushed aside." Her irritation was quickly outweighed by the need for sleep, and soon, Smokey felt her purrs reverberate on his back.

Stretched full-length under the two heat lamps, Chairman Meow heard it all.

Ungrateful young cubs, he thought. *I ought to get up and box both sets of those pert grey ears.* His eyes narrowed and he looked pensively out into the blackness of the winter storm. Did Misty still think that he went off just for the sheer pleasure of it? At least Smokey had some appreciation for Chairman's protection of their home.

A particularly violent gust of wind brought Chairman out of his reverie. He looked over his shoulder at Smokey and Misty; they both seemed deep in sleep. He yawned and stretched, then stepped out into the storm. It was more tolerable keeping watch over the property in summer, but there was to be no shirking, even in the bitter cold.

On the prairies in early winter, daylight is slow to arrive. The wind had finally died down, and the eastern sky was lined with pale pink and orange streaks. Misty awoke to the realization that she and Smokey were alone in the winter home. Stepping daintily over her brother, she sat directly underneath one of the heat lamps, feeling its warmth radiate down her back.

Sitting upright, it was almost too warm, and she turned to Smokey.

"Hey, wake up – breakfast time. The heat hog left."

Smokey opened one eye. "It's still way too early. The human won't be out to feed us for ages."

"Yeah, but it's a miserable morning. Maybe she'll bring our breakfast right out here. And maybe she'll even warm it up!"

"Spoiled much? Chairman said the human just did that for the older cats who lived here before us." Smokey rolled over, and kneaded the faded patchwork quilt that covered their cushions. "Lie down and catch a quick nap. You'll hear the human coming later."

Misty sighed, and thought about venturing out to sit before the sliding door and putting on her cute face. That was usually good for prompt food delivery and some attention. She ventured a little way out of the winter home.

Out of the glow of the heat lamps, the cold seeped quickly through her thick fur. She couldn't see lights or hear any activity in the house, so she turned around and scampered back to her brother. She nudged him with her head, and Smokey moved over to make room under the lamps.

Partially obscured behind a low snowdrift across the road, the cold yellow eyes of the large, coal-black cat followed their every movement. He would bide his time. For now.

Chairman picked his way through the fresh snow and weaved around broken tree branches. The wind was finally beginning to diminish. In the distance, he could see the warm glow of the heat lamps and picked up his pace in anticipation of their comfort.

It was during his walks around the property that Chairman most missed the older cats. Chuck, their faithful black guardian, who had entrusted him with the care of the remaining cats. Bandit, with her gentle spirit and her beautiful calico coat. Moonsie, with his wisdom, patience, and good fellowship. And always in the back of his mind, his sister, and the difficulty he continued to have in coming to grips with her loss.

Chairman had been slow to warm to the newcomers. The human had good intentions by bringing him companionship, but they just had so much to learn. He liked their given names, but it appeared they would have nicknames too. Ridiculous, really. The human rarely called Smokey by his real name, but his nickname, Lanky. And the little mouthy one? Smudgy. Chairman cracked a rusty smile. The name actually suited her, with her little pushed-in face.

He had never understood the need to give a cat a name that was completely beneath its dignity. Chairman Meow liked his name. It had stature – gravitas. The tall, young human who had given him his name knew how to interact with a cat too – no gushing, no mushy baby talk. He would sit down on the stairs of the deck, and Chairman would jump into his lap. No cuddling, no squeezing – just some gentle stroking down the back. It was all a cat needed. He didn't understand these young cats who felt the need to drape themselves all over a human whenever they had the opportunity or roll over onto their backs, exposing their soft, white underbellies for rubs.

One more prowl through the forest, he thought, *and I'll be ready for my breakfast and a nap.*

The familiar and lyrical cadence of "Kitties… kitty, kitty, kitties!" rang through the chill morning air. Misty periscoped up immediately and nudged her brother.

"Hey, it's breakfast – come on!" Perpetually active and always hungry, Misty dashed out of the winter home and skidded to a stop beside the food dish near the porch door. She called back over her shoulder to her brother. "You'd better hurry. It's roast beef scraps *and* they're warmed up!!"

Smokey, slower to wake, stretched leisurely and padded out of the comfort of the winter home. He picked his way through the fresh snow to the food dish and settled down to eat beside Misty. The warm scraps were welcome on this cold morning, and both cats enjoyed their breakfast. Piled beside the warmed scrap dish was a small mound of kibble. Smokey liked the warm scraps, but there was nothing wrong with the kibble either. The human knew which kind they liked best and ensured the supply was abundant.

"Where do you think Chairman went? I don't remember him leaving. Do you?" Misty asked through a mouthful of beef.

Smokey shook his head. "No, I don't. But he'll soon be back. It's too cold to be out for any length of time." The frantic chirping of the sparrows at the bird feeder brought both heads out of the dish, and two sets of grey ears snapped to attention. Chairman was following the path around the front of the deck and was obviously looking forward to his breakfast. Smokey had to give him credit: he didn't give them a hard time for eating what was put out if they got there first and didn't leave much for him.

Once at the food, Chairman licked the edge of the plate, scooping up the last fragments of the warmed beef and then turned to the pile of kibble. Crunching noises followed as he worked his way through a considerable amount of it.

"Where did you go?" Misty asked. Chairman picked his head up from his breakfast and gave her a level stare.

"Where do you think I go? We've had this conversation I don't know *how many* times. My job is to look after the property and to look after you."

Misty sighed and, with strained patience, retorted, "Yes, I know *that*. But were there any different places you went today? Or any different stray cats you saw?"

Chairman looked up from his kibble with the resignation of one whose repast was going to be continually interrupted. "I went out through the forest, over to the small barn, and around the bins. Then I walked through the pasture down to the edge of the creek. After that, I came back and took one more walk through the forest." He paused.

"What else?" Misty asked excitedly; she sensed that Chairman wasn't telling them everything.

"I smelled that ginger stray… and then I saw him in the distance beyond the small barn standing on a fallen tree. And there was one more…" Chairman looked at the remaining kibble, as if he no longer had an appetite, and slowly rose to his feet. "I don't want either of you two wandering anywhere near the outside of the property. Got it?"

Smokey nodded obediently. Chairman glared at Misty, and she dropped her gaze. She nodded reluctantly, and then trotted toward the base of the bird-feeder tree, watching intently as the sparrows tried to make inroads on the frozen suet in its swinging cage. Chairman and Smokey watched her attempts to stay absolutely still to catch an unwary bird off guard.

Smokey asked quietly, "Are you worried about that ginger stray?"

Chairman kept his gaze turned toward Misty. "No." He paused for a long moment. "Yes. He's persistent. He hasn't taken me seriously that I want him gone. I know he comes around late at night and I've smelled him in the garage near the cushions. Don't worry – I can deal with him. It's just that –" Chairman stopped abruptly.

Changing the subject, he pointed at Misty as she scooted up the bird-feeder tree and balanced with precision on the low branch where the suet cage swung, her eyes laser-focused on the sparrows just out of reach. "Where does she get the energy?" He tipped his head back and yawned widely. "I need some sleep. It was a long night."

Smokey agreed. "It was." His sister had scooted down the tree and was now racing back and forth between it and the tree closest to it, trying her best to catch a blue jay, which showed its disdain of her efforts with jeering squawks.

Chairman picked his way through the snow to the winter home and stretched out beneath the heat lamps. In seconds, he was asleep. Smokey padded up quietly, and as carefully as he could, stretched himself out alongside Chairman, wondering if he could ever be a guardian cat. It didn't seem likely. There was too much to learn – and too much that terrified him.

After the first storm of the season, the weather moderated. No additional snow fell to obscure tracks and trails, but the wind blew daily, blowing snow into low areas and piling up behind the cats' enclosure.

On warmer days, the cats sunned themselves on the deck, which had been cleared of snow for them, or napped on the cushions in the garage, which had been pulled forward to catch the warmth from the feeble rays of the winter sun. The human stayed outside with them regularly, making sure their food and water supply was abundant, and being available for lap time.

Chairman liked a *little* bit of lap time with the human. He considered it an obligation to show her some appreciation for her care. If the human held him too close or squeezed him too tightly, he pushed his head vigorously under her arm to let her know the terms of their arrangement. Close, but not too close. If Chairman had the lap, the newcomers, as he still referred to them sometimes, were not welcome, and he showed his displeasure with a swift slap to the offender's ears. When he was ready to be released, he would not-so-gently flex his claws into the human's leg, and at this point, he would be rapidly ejected.

Smokey especially loved lap time. He loved hugs, cuddles, squeezes, soft talking – all of it. He would tip up his face and nuzzle the human. She would touch her face to his, all the while admiring his beautiful fur and his gentlemanly deportment. Misty, on the other hand, disdained lap time altogether. She would condescend to be stroked with all four feet on the ground. However, she had discovered a trick with which the human was completely enamoured: rolling over on her back and letting the human rub her tummy. It was all Misty could do not to roll her eyes when the human cooed over her when her tummy was exposed.

In between patrols of the property, Chairman spent considerable time trying to teach his new charges different things they needed to know to keep safe and healthy. He described the purpose of the outdoor cooker, and the risks involved in careless leaps onto its lid, he reiterated the dangers of venturing too close to the creek until it was completely frozen over, and he sat up with them the first night a group of raccoons entered their garage, explaining why they should be given a wide berth.

Misty looked at the plump intruders with their identical facial markings. "Aww, they're cute. And so friendly!" she said, as the last one to leave gave her a big wave and a cheeky grin.

"They might look that way, but trust me – it's just better if you ignore them. Let them have the few scraps they're coming for and let that be the end of it," Chairman told her sternly. The raccoons came looking for scraps so often that their presence was no longer a novelty, and Misty eventually lost interest in them.

Chairman didn't tell the younger cats, but his interactions with the stray cats around the property were becoming more common, which was unusual during the colder weather. In most cases, however, those interactions amounted to a simple acknowledgement of his authority as the other cat stayed out of his path or bolted away. There was, however, one encounter that was more than a little bewildering.

One morning, Chairman stepped abruptly into a sheltered clearing outside of the property where the ginger stray was eating a small, mangled bird. Near the remnants of the bird were some scraps that had clearly been stolen from the house dishes.

The ginger stray tensed, ready for battle. For a long moment, Chairman glared at his long-time adversary. Technically, the ginger stray had a perfect right to be where he was. Grudgingly, Chairman acknowledged the fact. Finally, he spoke stiffly. "I'm interrupting your meal. I'll leave you alone." He turned to go.

The ginger stray got to his feet. "Wait! Can't we come to some sort of understanding here? I don't mean any harm to you or those two grey simpletons you somehow feel responsible for. All I'm looking for is a little occasional food I don't have to catch and kill for myself. Is that so unforgiveable?"

"Do you mean to say," Chairman said doubtfully, "that you aren't going to try to convince the… as you say… two grey simpletons to leave with you? Or try to take over our home?"

"Nothing of the sort," the ginger stray replied emphatically. "Just looking to supplement my diet. I'm not a young cat anymore, you know."

Chairman looked at him more closely. He had never had the leisure to scrutinize the other cat at such close proximity before, but now he could see some of the ravages of time and weather. The tips of both of the ginger stray's ears had been frostbitten, he had a vicious-looking wound on the side of his face, and his longer-haired fur showed a distinct lack of attention. For a brief second, Chairman regretted the threat he had issued long ago.

Bandit would have had her work cut out for her, taming that fur into some semblance of order, he thought wistfully and surprisingly.

Chairman snapped out of his memories and said, "If you can promise me you won't infringe on our home or hurt my family, then I think we can reach some sort of compromise."

"I agree. And thank you. I respect your interest in protecting your family." He looked off into the distance and continued quietly, "I couldn't protect mine."

Chairman looked up quickly, but the ginger stray turned his attention back to his breakfast, clearly not wanting to elaborate. He didn't look up as Chairman padded off, perplexed and unsettled.

What did he mean? Chairman thought. *What had happened to his family?*

After that day, Chairman and the ginger stray occasionally crossed paths, respecting each other's capabilities and space. Chairman sometimes spied him tucked up in the area between the rows of bales near the small barn, getting a drink at the cattle waterer, or prowling just outside the forest looking for his dinner. It appeared he was keeping his promise to stay away from Misty and Smokey, so Chairman reciprocated by occasionally bringing extra scraps to the outer edge of the forest and leaving them there. The ginger stray was true to his word, and gradually, Chairman's opinion of him shifted from one of distrust to one of respect.

Long after Chairman had left him to his breakfast, the ginger stray was still sitting in front of it, staring into the distance. He was usually able to keep memories of what had happened to his family at bay, but Chairman's commitment to the young cats in his care brought it all back. He shook his head, willing the memories away.

He had roamed widely as a young cat, glorying in his speed and strength. He never stayed in one spot for long and had learned early in life how to find food, whether it was food he caught himself or food he stole.

When a brutal late-winter storm caught him by surprise, he took shelter in a run-down barn. A few cats lived there, but from what he could see, they had to primarily fend for themselves. Often, there was a human around the site, but he offered them very little in the way of care or affection. Small amounts of hard food were occasionally thrown to them, over which the cats fought viciously. It was clear that this human had little liking for the cats, kicking them or throwing objects at them if he had the opportunity, barely tolerating them only because they kept the rodent population in check. Despite the harm that could come to him, the ginger stray returned to the barn regularly, as the winter was harsh and the barn provided some protection from the frigid wind.

One of the young cats, a small pregnant black and white female, befriended him as the long winter dragged on, sharing what little hard food she could get. As they grew more comfortable with each other, they spent the nights cuddled up together in the matted, rotten straw, combining their body heat. And she told him more about the cruelty of the human.

"Then why do you stay here when he neglects and mis-treats everyone?"

"It's all I know," she said quietly. "I was born here."

The ginger stray looked at her carefully. "What about the rest of your family? Where are they?"

"They ran away, because they were terrified of what might happen to them."

"Why didn't you leave too? Leave with them?"

"I would have, but I was out hunting when they left. I was so hungry, I just had to go. And I didn't know where they went – I didn't know which way to go to find them. So, I stayed. I was scared to go anywhere by myself. " She looked fondly at her new friend. "I'm not as scared now."

As the winter waned, the little female's pregnancy became more evident. She was terrified and expressed her fears to her friend.

"When I have kittens, I'm afraid what might happen to them," she told him anxiously late one night. "That human will hurt them, I know it."

"Not if I can help it. When it's warmer and you feel it's getting close to your time, we'll get you away from here, and you and your kittens will be safe." With their plans in place, the two cats looked forward to spring.

To supplement the little female's food supply, the ginger stray hunted for them both. He brought her back his catches and watched in satisfaction as she tore into the food. She looked healthier; her eyes were brighter and her coat, shinier.

One early spring morning, he set out on an extended prowl. He needed to bring back something substantial for the little female so she would have the energy to travel. He was also looking for a place of security and safety for her to have her kittens. In a grove of leafless trees, he discovered a fallen log with one end hollowed out. *That will do nicely,* he thought in satisfaction.

Once a birthing site had been located, he turned his attention to hunting. He discovered a nest of field mice, killed three of them quickly, and ate one. Carrying the remaining two in his mouth, he trotted swiftly back to the dilapidated barn.

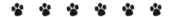

Oh no, oh no, the little female thought desperately. *Not now, not yet.* But the strong urges in her lower body could not be slowed or denied. Crawling into a stained and overturned pail, she felt the overpowering need to push and watched in despair as one kitten was born. Two more were born in rapid succession. She ripped the membranes from them hurriedly and looked around frantically for a more secluded place. *Where can I go? Where can I take them?*

The barn door was wrenched open, and a tiny mew from one of the kittens caused the angry human to look down. With a curse, he scowled at the terrified little cat and her new family. He roughly picked up the pail by the handle, sliding the new mother and her kittens to its bottom with a heart-rending thud. He carried the pail outside, tossed it carelessly in the back of a truck, climbed in, and drove away from the barn.

As the ginger stray got closer to the barn, he could hear the cries of his friend, in addition to tiny kitten cries. He quickly narrowed down the source of those cries to the back of the angry human's truck. He watched in panic as the truck sped down the road and turned down a much less-travelled trail toward the pond. The ginger stray raced after them, tearing through leafless tree rows and flattened grasses, taking a shorter path to the same destination.

The truck slammed to a stop, and the angry human climbed out. From his vantage point at the edge of the trees, the ginger stray watched in horrified disbelief as the angry human removed a sack from the back of the truck and set a large rock in it. As he casually reached into the pail, and tossed both mother and babies into the sack, the furious cat was galvanized into action. He sprinted out of the trees as the angry human tied a knot in the neck of the sack.

Suddenly, the angry human reared back, as the ginger stray leaped up – a clawing, scratching, biting, screaming fury. Stunned, he released the sack and frantically tried to grab his assailant, finally getting hold of the cat's scruff. He threw it angrily to the ground, where its head struck the gravel. It lay still.

Wincing at the scratches on his neck and chest, the angry human returned to his truck and clutched the sack. Frantic meows could be heard within it. Disregarding the pleas for mercy, the angry human stalked to the edge of the pond, drew back, and flung the sack. The sack rested briefly on the thin layer of ice and then sank under the water's surface.

Satisfied, he strolled back to his truck and spun away, narrowly missing the ginger stray and spraying him with small gravel stones. The small stones pelting his body roused the cat from his stupor. Disregarding the pain in his head, he sat up and looked across the pond. Tiny bubbles rose to the surface where the sack had been thrown.

Ignoring the frigid water and the dagger-like ice crystals, he plunged into the pond, keeping his vision focused on the position of the bubbles. Dropping his face into the murky water, he could see the sack where it rested on the pond bottom not far below him. There was frantic movement inside the sack, which gradually slowed and then stopped altogether.

He swam slowly to the edge of the pond and flung himself on the dead grass. He was appalled at the cruelty he had just witnessed, but most of all, he was heart-sick at his inability to help his friend.

Taking a deep breath, the ginger stray roused himself from the traumatic memories of the past. Even though it had happened a long time ago, he had not forgiven himself for the deaths of his friend and her kittens. His hatred of humans had intensified over time, surpassed only by his loathing for himself.

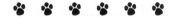

The brief winter daylight was fading quickly, and the wind was bitterly cold. Chairman picked up his pace – his patrol had been uneventful, and he was looking forward to the comfort of their winter home and a warm supper. Without warning, he heard a sneering voice behind him.

"What's your hurry? Let me guess. I'll bet you want to get back to that pretty little warm house and your pretty little companions."

Chairman wheeled around. The force of the wind had masked the presence of the large, coal-black cat, who stood a few paces away. His condescending comments raised the fur on Chairman's back. He opened his mouth to retort, but the black cat continued speaking, his cold yellow eyes narrowing.

"I've seen you around here, and I think it's about time you were told: this is *my* property and you would do well to stay off it." The black cat's eyes flashed at Chairman, daring him to react or to contradict him in any way.

"Oh, and another thing. Those two pretty little companions of yours. You'd do better to stay home and watch over them. Who knows what could happen to them when you're not around?"

Chairman's eyes narrowed, his ears flattened, and he crouched down, tail lashing. "You've got some nerve – threatening young cats who can't defend themselves. If I ever catch you near them, I will kill you. And that is a promise."

The black cat smiled. The gesture was sinister. "I'd like to see you try, you pampered, useless –"

Chairman flew at the black cat, interrupting the insults about to be delivered. They thrashed in the deep snow, a spitting, snarling, yowling, clawing, biting blur. Chairman caught his opponent's front paw in his mouth and bit down hard. The black cat screamed in surprise and pain, and briefly let go of his grip on the side of Chairman's neck.

Chairman seized his opportunity, twisted quickly, and sank his teeth into the other cat's throat. He bit down harder and could taste warm blood. Visions of Smokey and Misty being terrorized by this monster gave him strength.

I'm going to end him, he thought coldly. *I just have to hang on a little longer.*

The black cat lay motionless, his blood staining the snow red. The battle finished, Chairman eased his grip on his opponent's neck and got to his feet, gasping for breath. He looked down briefly to assess his own injuries.

His brief inattention was all the black cat needed. In a burst of speed, he flew out of the snow and captured Chairman by the throat. His teeth sank deeper, deeper, while Chairman kicked at the other cat's stomach with his waning strength.

I can't die like this, he thought in panic. *What will happen to –*

A streak of orange shot past his blurring vision and broadsided the black cat. Chairman felt the black cat's grip wrenched from his throat, and in astonishment, he watched in shock as the ginger stray and the black cat grappled almost silently to the death in the snow. With lightning fast slashes, the ginger stray tore open a second wound in the black cat's neck, spraying the snow with blood. The black cat clutched at his throat, staggered back, and fell. He did not get up.

The ginger stray swiftly turned his attention to Chairman. "How bad is it? Other than your throat, where else? *Where else?*"

Chairman opened his mouth to reply and found that he couldn't. The pain in his throat supressed his speech and his stomach ached fiercely. He tried again, opening his mouth, and leaning forward as if to force the words out. His unlikely rescuer looked at him in consternation.

"We need to get you somewhere to rest. Do you think you can walk?"

Chairman nodded. He took a few tentative steps and found walking manageable.

"Come with me then." The ginger stray turned and trotted toward the rows of bales near the small barn. He looked back at Chairman, weaving unsteadily on his feet. In a few strong leaps, he was back at Chairman's side. "I'll stay with you. One step at a time."

Together, they made their halting way toward both shelter and further reconciliation.

For three days, Chairman lay in the protective shelter of the space between the straw bales. Snow was unable to make its way inside, and the ginger stray had clawed away at the sides of the bales to make a comfortable bed. Chairman found that the pains in his stomach had eased somewhat, but he could feel open wounds on his neck and his chest. His voice had still not returned, so he couldn't express his gratitude to his rescuer for the shelter and his concern.

The ginger stray brought him tidbits from the scrap dishes to eat, but they lay untouched. He wanted to ask about Misty and Smokey and whether they were alarmed about his absence, but couldn't.

On the morning of the fourth day, the ginger stray stood looking over Chairman as he slept restlessly, shivering with cold and fever.

There's nothing more I can do for him, he thought wearily. *It's time he went home.*

He nudged Chairman gently; he didn't stir. In alarm, the ginger stray pushed on Chairman's tender stomach with one paw. Chairman winced and opened his eyes. The ginger stray looked at him gravely.

"I think it's time I helped you get home. You need your human's help."

Chairman opened his mouth to reply but could say nothing. He nodded briefly and got unsteadily to his feet. Slowly, they made their way from the shelter of the bales and back to the winter home.

"*Where have you been?* We've been so worried about you!" Smokey exclaimed as Chairman staggered into the winter home. Behind Chairman stood the ginger stray. In alarm, Smokey asked, "What happened? Your throat –"

"Before you ask," the ginger stray interrupted, "I didn't do it. It was another cat altogether. But he won't cause you any problems." He paused. "He's dead. He and your friend got into a fight. Your friend was hurt, so I finished the job."

For once in her short life, Misty had nothing to say. The ginger stray explained tersely, "He's been resting with me for the last few days, but he needs human help. He's very weak and he hasn't eaten. And those wounds on his throat need tending." He looked down at Chairman, shivering under the heat lamps. "You need to get your human to see him. Now. *Now!*"

Galvanized into action, Smokey and Misty leaped through the deep snow and up onto the deck. They meowed loudly in front of the sliding door and stood up on their back feet, pawing frantically at the glass for the human.

From the safety of the trees, the ginger stray waited until the human had seen the other cats, waited until he heard the door open and slam, and waited until he watched the cats bring the human to their injured friend's side. Only then did he turn and pad slowly back to his shelter in the bales.

The human placed Chairman gently in the carrier and took him away in the car. Misty and Smokey watched anxiously as the car rounded the bend and the sound of its tires crunching in the snow had faded.

"He's going to the vet," Misty pronounced knowledgeably. "He'll get some little bits that the human with the deep voice will put in his throat, and he'll soon be all better. You'll see!"

Smokey wasn't as optimistic. He had seen the look on the ginger stray's face as Chairman had staggered into the winter home. And even though the wounds on his neck looked frightening, Smokey sensed there was something else wrong. But to keep Misty reassured, he replied with as much enthusiasm as he could muster, "Of course, he will. He'll be back in no time. It will all be fine."

It will all be fine, he repeated to himself. *I hope it will all be fine.* Together, the two cats climbed back into the winter home to await Chairman's return. Smokey napped lightly, but Misty was wide awake.

He has to be all right, Misty thought in rising panic, *or what am I going to do? I know I complain about him all the time, but I don't want him to be gone. He has to come back. He just has to.*

Three lifetimes later, the car pulled back into the driveway in front of the garage. Misty poked Smokey to wake him.

"He's back! Chairman's back! See, I told you it was all going to be fine!" The human took the carrier to the winter home and lifted Chairman gently out of it, placing him directly under the heat lamps.

Wide-eyed, Misty didn't protest. She watched as the human smoothed out the quilts around Chairman and tucked a corner over his back. The human left and returned shortly with a tiny bit of warmed food on a plate. She held it up to Chairman's mouth. He opened his eyes briefly and gave the food a tentative lick; his head sank back down to rest between his paws.

Misty and Smokey settled themselves near Chairman, not touching him but close by so he would know they were there. The routine of the next few days unfolded: the human would take Chairman into the house briefly – "He's getting his little bits to make him better," Misty stated emphatically – then he would be brought back to the winter home to rest.

As Chairman's condition worsened, it became clear to Smokey and Misty just how important they all were to the human. She would kneel in the snow near Chairman in the winter home, stroking his fur and speaking to him in low, comforting tones. She would pick him up carefully and carry him into the house for longer periods of time. Smokey and Misty wondered uneasily about Chairman's absence, as he would, under normal circumstances, never consider spending time there.

One bitterly cold morning, the human appeared at the entrance of the enclosure much earlier than she normally did. Misty was ready to purr for breakfast, but something on the human's face stopped her. The human put her head down near Chairman and whispered softly to him. Her face was red and blotchy, and she seemed to have trouble breathing. She stroked Chairman's emaciated body softly and, ever so gently, lifted him up.

The human carried Chairman into the house for what would be the last time. She laid him down carefully on a soft blanket, and knelt beside him. She whispered to him and ran her hand gently down his back over and over again. Chairman felt her deep love for him. He knew she didn't want his life to end like this. He tried to lift his head and tell her with his eyes; he had grown too weak to purr.

Morning was beginning to break when the human with the deep voice carried Chairman outside. Misty and Smokey watched as Chairman was placed gently on the front seat of the truck. Before the door was closed, Chairman turned his head toward them. His eyes told them what his voice could not. Be careful. Be grateful.

They watched the truck drive away, around the bend in the road. In the silence, they could hear the crunch of the truck tires on the snow recede in the distance.

"Is he going back to the vet?" Smokey asked, wide-eyed.

Misty shook her head. "I don't know. Maybe. But he wasn't in the –"

A single gunshot rang out in the frigid air, echoing through the stillness of the morning. The birds at the feeder were silent.

I had taken a picture of Chairman a year earlier – in the photo, he is standing on top of the cats' winter home. He is not looking at me, but at a point off in the distance. In his prime, he is dapper, majestic, and fearless. I carried that picture of him in my mind during the last days of his life, and the contrast between the two images was heartbreaking.

Making the choice to end Chairman's life was incredibly difficult. I agonized over that decision for two days, but in the end, I realized it was selfish of me to keep him alive for my own sake. A week's worth of medication had made no difference to his condition, and his quality of life had diminished rapidly. His needs had to come before mine. Doing the right thing – the responsible thing – was not the easy thing.

Misty and Smokey couldn't go back inside their winter home. It smelled of Chairman – his healthy smell as well as his sickness. In his illness, he had soiled their blankets. The heat lamps seemed to amplify the smell. In spite of the cold, they slept on their summer cushions and huddled close together as the nighttime temperature plummeted.

The next morning, the human caught them still asleep on the summer cushions and realized something was preventing them from sleeping in greater comfort. She removed the soiled bedding from the enclosure and turned their cushions. She brought them a fresh quilt and spread it carefully over the cushions, keeping its edges away from the heat lamps.

When she had finished, she remained on her knees in the snow, looking inside the enclosure. Smokey leaned in and placed his front paws on her knee. She gathered him in close and hugged him. He tipped up his head and touched his nose to hers.

From his vantage point on a fallen log deep in the forest, the ginger stray watched it all, suddenly feeling envious of the care and affection the young cats seemed to take as a matter of course.

As the winter days dragged on, the absence of Chairman Meow weighed heavily on Misty and Smokey. For all her complaining about his overbearing attitude and his tendency to hog the heat, Misty realized that the only reason she felt safe romping about the property, and chasing birds and squirrels in every direction, was because Chairman was there. He had been the constant in their short lives and now he was gone. She didn't feel nearly as warm in the winter home, even though she was now able to lie directly under the heat lamps.

If Misty was unsettled, Smokey was unstrung. Every unfamiliar noise alarmed him. When meals were brought to them, he couldn't relax and enjoy them. His ears were constantly at attention. At night in their enclosure, all he could think about were the hazards just beyond the warm glow of their heat lamps. He remained awake for hours at night and napped throughout the day. The human grew alarmed at his lethargy, not understanding its origin. She brought him tasty tidbits, some of which he ate dutifully, but it all tasted the same.

Weeks after Chairman's death, Smokey was still edgy. Staying awake at night and sporadically napping throughout the day was taking its toll on both cats. One day, Misty finally lost all patience with him.

"Look, you have to get a grip on yourself! You panic when you hear a mouse. As soon as you see the human, you practically climb her legs to get into her arms. You're a wreck!"

On the cushions, Smokey stared at her, bleary-eyed, as her rant continued.

"I know what happened to Chairman was terrible, but you can't go through the rest of your life scared of what might happen. There've been no threats to us here – we're safe!"

Smokey lifted his head. "I know everything you're saying is true, but I just can't..." His voice trailed off in shame. "If I could just relax and sleep –" He yawned, tilting his head back, back, and looking up...

"There!" he exclaimed. "*That's* the solution to my problem!"

"What on *earth* are you talking about?" Misty asked.

"Up there." He pointed. "If I could get up there to sleep, no one would be able to get at me." Misty tried to follow the direction of his long, grey limb. He hopped off the cushions and dragged her toward the front of the garage; he pointed again. "Look – one of the young humans left something up there – I can see it! I can sleep on that!"

Misty looked upward at a cloth-like object hanging over the top of the raised garage door. She shook her head. "And just how do you propose to get up there?" she asked caustically. "And even if you could, think about this: if *you* can get up there, so could someone else."

Smokey's enthusiasm for his loft-y slumber idea came crashing down. Misty was raising valid points. How *was* he going to get up there? But... *if* he could, it would hopefully be too much work for someone else.

Misty chuckled. "It won't work. And you'll break all your legs trying. And even if, by some chance, you happen to get up, how will you get down?" She shook her head again and stalked out of the garage.

Smoked glared at her retreating figure. "Just you wait and see."

Looking back over her shoulder, she called, "I'll leave you to it then. I have better things to do than watch you make a fool of yourself." She paused. "You'll end up at the vet clinic – you'll see!"

With more enthusiasm than he had felt for a long time, Smokey clutched one of the cushions in his mouth and dragged it into position below the raised garage door.

"So, if I fall," he said to the pair of sparrows watching his every move from the safety of the rafters, "I won't hurt myself." Satisfied with the precautions he had taken, Smokey leaped up onto the lid of the outdoor cooker. He remembered just in time he should have checked if it was hot.

Fortunately, it was not. He gathered his legs underneath him, shifting back and forth, and sprang. His front paws caught the edge of the door, but his back legs failed to gain traction. He pedalled wildly for a few seconds, the sparrows twittering in gentle amusement at his predicament.

"Oh, shut up, you feathery —" His insult was cut short as his front paws lost their grip, and he fell awkwardly to the cushion below. The sparrows twittered louder, clearly overjoyed at his clumsiness.

Okay, so that *plan isn't going to work,* he thought in resignation. On the rafters, the birds watched closely to see what his next move would be.

His next move was interrupted by the unwelcome arrival of the human. Seeing that the cats' cushion was out of place, she pulled it back deep into the garage, out of the blast of the cold winds.

Arrrgh, why did you do that? he growled impatiently. For the first time ever, Smokey rejected her invitation to cuddle. *Just get going!* he thought. *I have things to do and a loft to claim.* Impatiently, he watched her set down some fresh kibble and lunch leftovers. She tried again to entice him to cuddle, but he bolted out of the garage and under the car.

From his vantage point under the car, Smokey saw her legs walk to the porch door. It opened and the legs went inside. He darted out from underneath the car to ponder his next move. Three more sparrows had joined their friends on the rafters to watch his performance.

Nothing better to do, Smokey thought in disgust, *than watch me make a fool of myself?* The sparrows fluffed their feathers and twittered with anticipation.

He critically examined the assorted cupboards and storage shelves scattered around the garage. There was nothing available that would be a direct leap to his loft. Unless...

Smokey eyed the old kitchen cabinets that were unevenly stacked on top of one another. If he timed it just right, he should be able to jump from on top of *those*, right onto the track that supported the door. And victory would be his! The timing would be critical and his balance would have to be perfect. Or else he would be on the garage floor again, with an even larger contingent of sparrows witnessing his humiliation.

Safety first, he thought, as he dragged the cushion back underneath the door once again. Gathering his nerve, he leaped onto the kitchen cupboards. So far, so good. Carefully stretching up on his back legs, he could see the dust coating the door track.

That could be a problem, he thought, *so I'll have to compensate for that.*

Shifting from foot to foot, and accompanied by both excited and scornful sparrow twittering, he leaped up onto the track. It was narrow, and as he had predicted, heavy with dust. One foot slipped, but he was able to correct his balance and stepped from the track onto the back of the door. Disappointed that the show was over, the sparrows flew away.

Hah! Smokey thought smugly. *And they thought I couldn't do it!* Now that he was up here, he thought he recognized what it was that had been resting on the top of the door. It looked like something he remembered Chairman telling them about: when Chuck was a young cat, he would sit with the younger human in this tent-like structure pretending to hide from the deer.

Looking around, however, he wondered if he had inherited a private furnished loft or a multi-bird family rest stop. Bird droppings as well as bat droppings peppered the top of the fabric. It felt a little like their quilt, but was slippery and a little bouncy. The droppings problem was easily resolved by a few sweeps of his paw.

This will do quite nicely, he thought smugly as he stretched out. Between his many sleepless nights, and his mental and physical exertion in figuring out a way to get up here, he fell asleep almost immediately.

It was almost dark when the evening birdsong woke him. Smokey stretched luxuriously, feeling more rested already. Suddenly, he realized he hadn't worked out a way to get down from his perch. Frowning, he peered over the edge of the door. The garage floor looked a long way down. And drat the human – she had moved that blasted cushion *again!*

Stepping out carefully onto the track, he balanced there and, more carefully still, leaned over and pointed himself toward the cupboards. He landed on their top successfully, and from there, it was two easy jumps to the floor.

Misty strolled into the garage just as he made his triumphant leap down. "So, I see you haven't broken anything. Surprising, really."

Smokey smirked at her. "Want to join me next time?"

"Not a chance. Scared of heights now," she admitted. "I'll stick to the lower altitudes."

As winter crept toward spring, Smokey spent his nights and naps in his loft. Even though he was sometimes chilly, he felt it was a small price to pay for being able to sleep peacefully. He tried to cajole Misty, daring her even, to make the leap to loft living, but she would have none of it. Without Smokey beside her in the winter home, Misty spent her time on the summer cushions.

Since they were no longer using the winter home, the human with the deep voice dismantled it, wondering why they had suddenly deserted it. Misty and Smokey watched its decommissioning with little regret. It was a reminder of Chairman's death, and they were glad to see it gone.

On a raw early-spring morning, Misty and Smokey cuddled together on the summer cushions. A combination of ice and snow was hitting the side of the garage with tiny metallic sounds. They watched lazily as the human arrived with their breakfast. They could smell that it was warmed and that it would be tasty, but they weren't hungry enough to pull themselves away from the comfort provided by their cushions. The human bent over them to check that they were warm and then disappeared inside the house.

"Well, so much for the loving when the weather gets foul," Misty muttered.

"Oh, give it up. It isn't even that cold." Smokey got to his feet with a shivering stretch and ambled toward their breakfast. "If you want it while it's warm, you'd better roll out. I think it's the stuff I smelled through the windows yesterday."

Misty rose to her feet and had a long, luxurious stretch. The foot that had been injured felt a little stiff on cold, damp days, but once she was up and moving, the stiffness abated. She disdained breakfast in favour of venturing out of the shelter of the garage.

The snow was getting deeper, and the wind was stronger; she could see there would be no entertainment at the bird-feeder tree today. She sighed, wondering what on earth there would be to do other than nap today. A sudden gust of wind almost pushed her off her feet. She could barely see across the road.

Yeah, she thought, *maybe napping isn't the worst thing I could be doing.* She turned back inside the garage toward breakfast, which was now gone.

"Ya snooze, ya lose," Smokey said amiably, back on his cushions and in the process of grooming the fur on a long back leg. "But hey, there's some kibble left." He gestured at the pile, which was now lightly snow-covered. Misty tapped disinterestedly at the kibble pile with a front paw to dislodge the snow.

Smokey suddenly snapped to attention, his back leg sticking straight up in front of him. "Did you hear that?"

"What? All I hear is the…" The wind abated for a brief moment, and both cats could hear it. Another cat. And it was close by.

"It's gotta be a stray. What are we going to do?" Smokey realized he still had his leg in the air and tucked it down. The question was answered for him, as a small, snow-covered object staggered into the garage. It walked a few paces farther and then collapsed.

Misty tiptoed closer. "It's not moving. Maybe it died." She touched her nose to the visitor's fur and jumped back. "Nope, still alive."

"Well, what now? You remember what Chairman told us about stray cats. Well, about some of them, anyway." Smokey looked at the unconscious cat with amazement tinged with caution. "How did it manage to find us through this storm?"

"I don't know," Misty answered. "But I don't think it's a threat. Look how small it is. Come on – help me get it onto our cushions."

Together, Smokey and Misty tugged carefully on the frozen fur of the little cat and pulled it slowly onto their cushions. Most of the snow fell off during the process, and they could see that it had tabby-coloured markings; one ear showed evidence of frostbite. It was very thin and its eyes were closed tight.

"I think we'd better try to keep it warm," Misty said quietly. "You lie down on this side, and I'll lie down over here." They settled themselves on either side of the severely chilled little cat. The cold from its body seeped into them, and they tried to imagine what it would have been like, out there in the storm with nowhere to go and no one to look after them. The thought was sobering.

The storm continued throughout the day. Snow piled up in front of the garage, blowing off its roof, and swirling in intricate designs. The little cat showed no signs of recovery. The two older cats kept watch, staying close to its side.

At dark, the human came out to check on them for the night, and brought them a warm supper and more kibble. She didn't stay long enough to notice the additional body on the cushions and quickly went back inside. Misty and Smokey got up stiffly. Supper smelled good – it had been a long day keeping the stranger warm. They bent their heads to the food dish and tucked in.

"Any left for me?" A tiny voice came from the cushions they had just vacated. The little cat stood up shakily, and as it did, they could see it was much closer to kittenhood than adulthood.

"Come on over," Misty invited. "It's a little chilly closer to the opening, but some warm food will make a big difference." The kitten crept near as though drawn to the dish on an invisible string. Once there, it dropped its head and hoovered up the warm scraps.

Misty and Smokey watched with amusement as the kitten climbed right into the dish to get more. Its little face smeared with gravy, the kitten sighed with satisfaction. "I can't remember the last time I ate."

"I can see that," Smokey said. "So, now that you've come back from the brink, what's your story?"

The kitten trotted back to the cushions and climbed into the middle as if it had been there forever. It attempted to groom its fur, but settled for a quick face wash. Misty and Smokey joined it on the cushions, and all three cats made themselves comfortable.

"My mom and I were trying to get back to our barn. We were out hunting, or rather, she was trying to teach me a few things about hunting. We could sense that the storm was coming, but my mom wanted to stay out a little longer. Then the snow started, and the wind got really bad, and my mom and I got separated. I couldn't see her. I called and called for her, and I don't know where she is…" The kitten took a deep breath. "I was so cold and I couldn't see where I was going. The wind was so strong, I couldn't smell anything familiar."

Smokey encouraged, "And then what happened?"

"I had to keep moving because standing still or lying down would have meant I'd get too cold to ever move again. So I just went where the wind pushed me. I walked and walked and walked. When the wind went down a little, I could see this building, so I came this way." The kitten paused. "Thanks for helping me get warm and sharing your food."

Misty replied, "There's nothing much we can do tonight. It's too miserable to go anywhere. It's too bad our winter home was taken down – a night under a heat lamp would warm you through to your bones. But you'll have to make do with us."

"I don't know what a heat lamp is." The kitten snuggled closer to Smokey. "We all sleep out in a big barn and keep each other warm. I like to be close to other cats." Exhausted from its adventures, the kitten yawned widely and tucked its head down beside its little paws. Soon, Smokey felt its gentle purrs resonating on his stomach. He stretched out a long front limb and gathered the kitten in closer. Misty shook her head indulgently.

"Look at you, all sappy and taking care of the baby. Who would have ever thought you'd be doing something like that?"

Smokey looked at Misty thoughtfully. "I'm just beginning to wonder about some of the things Chairman told us. You know, about strays? Maybe he was wrong."

Misty looked down at the small form. It had rolled over and its little head was tucked right under Smokey's chin. "Maybe he was wrong about a lot of things."

Things generally look brighter in the morning – unless you're in the middle of a three-day snowstorm. Smokey stirred first. Snow had drifted farther into the garage and coated the side of their cushions closest to the opening. On the edge of sleep, he forgot for a moment what had happened, but then he felt the kitten knead its little paws gently into his stomach.

It's kind of a cute little thing, he thought paternally.

As if the kitten knew it was being watched, its eyes popped open. For a second, it looked disoriented, as if it, too, had forgotten where it was. Then it bounced up, licked one of Smokey's ears, and bounded off the cushions with its skinny tail sticking straight up in the air.

"Hey, just where do you think you're going?" Smokey asked. "No one's going anywhere right now. Take a look out there." The kitten stopped on its way to the opening. It looked miniscule beside the snowdrift, which was now taller than Smokey could stretch. "You're just going to have to stay with us until the snow stops. Then, we'll try and get you back to your mom."

The kitten made a comical attempt to climb the snowbank; it dug its claws into the snow, held on briefly, and then slid down and landed on its backside. It tried one more time before realizing that the effort was fruitless. Tired out now from its efforts, the kitten scampered back to Smokey and the warmth of the cushions.

Misty leaped over the snow at the entrance and shook the excess from her fur before stepping on the cushions.

"Where were you?" Smokey asked. "I don't imagine there were any birds at the feeder this morning. What else could have dragged you out in the snow?"

Misty began to groom her wet fur. "Just taking a look around. I was curious about where the ginger stray lived. I know Chairman used to leave food for him near the far edge of the forest, so I left some there for him this morning. Then, I climbed one of the trees at the near edge to see if he would come and get it. He did, finally, and then I followed him to see where he went."

Smokey asked, "Are you sure that was a smart thing to do? Just because he promised Chairman he wouldn't hurt us doesn't mean he's still going to honour that agreement."

"I don't think he saw me," Misty replied, "and even if he did, I don't think he means either of us any harm. If he really wanted to, he could have come here any time and hurt us both." She glanced at the kitten, snuggled up against Smokey's warm stomach again. "How's the young one today?"

"Wanted to go look for his mom and tried to climb over the snow over there to get the process started." Smokey chuckled indulgently. "But I convinced him it's going to have to wait for a bit."

"Well, once it's a little nicer out there, we can both try to get him home. I hope he has some idea about where he's going. I don't know how well his directionality will be working, and I think he got pretty disoriented in that storm."

"One thing at a time," Smokey said, as the human struggled to scale the snow at the entrance to the garage, their breakfast in hand. He casually draped a long limb over the kitten and cuddled it close, trying to keep it from the human's sight, and casually rearranged his body to hide it even more. Misty saw what he was doing and trotted over to the human to distract her. Two belly rubs later, the human hurried back into the house.

"Whew, that was close!" Smokey exclaimed.

"What was up with *that*? Why are you trying to hide it? You know the human would never hurt it."

"I'm just thinking about the kitten. If he lives where they don't have a lot of human contact, there's no point in him getting used to it. And if he isn't going to be here very long, there's also no point in the human making a fuss over him. We'll just try to keep him out of sight until we can get him out of here."

Misty nodded. His remarks made sense. The two cats took turns eating their breakfast, leaving one of them behind on the cushions to keep the kitten warm. They spent the rest of the day lazily napping, watching the kitten explore their garage, and answering its endless questions.

Misty opened her eyes. Directly in front of her face was a tiny pair of eyes, a wet black nose and long white whiskers. She reared back. "What do you think you're doing?" she asked with amusement.

The kitten held his position. "Getting ready to go home. See? It's not snowing now, so can we go? *Puuulllease?* I know my mom will be worried about me." A glance out the front of the garage confirmed the kitten's statement.

"You're right. But I have to ask you. Do you think you have any idea which way we're supposed to go to find your mom and the barn you all sleep in?"

The kitten nodded. "I do. I've got a really good direction-er. My mom told me I did."

"Well, let's hope you're right." Smokey entered the garage by way of the path the human made the evening before. "But first, we have to wait for a warm breakfast. And *you* – you'll have to get out of sight."

The opening of the porch door signalled the imminent arrival of the human. Smokey quickly pushed the kitten behind the outdoor cooker. It looked in hungry amazement at the pile of food and kibble left for them and pranced in excitement.

Once the human had returned to the house, Smokey said, "All right, young one – come and get it!" The kitten trotted over and put its two front feet right in the dish. Misty and Smokey looked at each other over its head.

"You're not starving today and you still have no manners. You should maybe tell your mom to rectify that little oversight," Misty told the back of the kitten's head.

The kitten lifted its head and waved a paw. "Yup, I can do that." Its head dropped back down into the dish, and all the older cats heard was its chomps and slurps of satisfaction.

Kittens, Misty thought. *You have to teach them everything.* She remembered how Chairman had gone through the same rituals with her and Smokey, and with a pang of guilt, realized she could have been much more cooperative.

The kitten lifted its head, finally full. "That was really good. I could get used to this."

Brought out of her reverie, Misty chuckled. "Sorry, young one. This human is ours. We're going to get you back with the cats you know. They'll be missing you."

"I suppose so," the kitten said regretfully, "but you've been really good to me. Thank you for looking after me."

Smokey smiled at the kitten, who was looking up at them trustingly. "Don't thank us too soon. We haven't got you home yet."

Together, all three stepped through the path made by the human and pushed through the snow to the road. The kitten sniffed the air, lifting its tiny nose as it stood up on its back legs. It breathed deeply and then dropped down on all fours again. "This way!" it said confidently.

Trotting down the path made by the truck's tires, all three headed west, with the two older cats following the kitten. It got sidetracked often, stopping to sniff discoloured snow or playing with small stones dislodged by the tires. Misty sighed. The day was passing quickly, with no sign of the "big barn" mentioned by the kitten.

"Are you sure you know where you're going?" she finally asked.

The kitten stopped and stretched up on its back legs again to sniff the air. It walked ahead three paces and stretched up again. Then, it backtracked underneath Smokey's belly and stretched up to sniff there. The two older cats watched its attempts to navigate.

"You're lost," Misty stated.

The kitten drooped, tired and confused. "I guess I am. I thought my direction-er would work better than this, but the snow is making it hard for me to smell much of anything."

Daylight was waning, so the older cats made the decision to return to their own home. "You'll have to come back with us, and we'll try again another day." Misty said.

The way back seemed much longer, and it was almost dark before they could see the garage. The older cats picked up their pace in anticipation of their cushions and something to eat, with the kitten lagging behind. Finally, Smokey picked it up by its scruff and carried it the rest of the way.

Entering the garage, they could sense they weren't alone. The ginger stray was crouched in front of the kibble, crunching loudly. He looked up as Smokey gently set the kitten down.

"Sorry – no one was here, so I thought you wouldn't mind."

Smokey looked at him cautiously. "It's… it's fine."

"So, who do we have here?" The ginger stray looked at the kitten with interest.

"Well, this one wandered in during the storm, half-starved and lost. We were trying to get it back to its mother, but I don't know how reliable its sense of direction is. I think it would get lost in this garage." Smokey shook his head indulgently. In his heart, he was glad the kitten might be staying. They would figure out how to introduce it to the human and –

The ginger stray interrupted Smokey's musings. "I get the sense that these two," he said to the kitten, and gesturing toward Smokey and Misty, "don't really want you around here."

Smokey opened his mouth to protest. But the kitten looked up at the ginger stray. "They never said that, and they let me have their food and looked after me when I –"

"Perhaps," the ginger stray interrupted, "but they already have each other, an established routine, and a human. I've got an idea. They have each other, and I have no one. What would you think about coming to stay with me until the snow melts, and then, if you want, we can find your home?"

To Smokey's dismay, the kitten bounded over to the ginger stray and snuggled between his front legs. *That's my kitten,* Smokey thought sadly. The ginger stray looked up, his eyes meeting Smokey's, and suddenly, Smokey remembered something Chairman had said after he and the ginger stray had reached a compromise. In some way, the ginger stray had been unable to protect his family. Another one of Chairman's admonitions crumbled, as Smokey understood the ginger stray was lonely and obviously needed someone to care for.

Realizing what he had to do, Smokey spoke up enthusiastically. "That sounds like a great idea! When the snow is gone, everything will be easier."

The ginger stray telegraphed his thanks to Smokey. He shepherded the kitten toward the kibble and encouraged it to eat. Then, the kitten and his new guardian rounded the corner of the garage and disappeared into the darkness. Brooding, Smokey walked to the cushions and turned his face away.

Misty opened her mouth to say something but then changed her mind. Quietly, she padded out toward the bird-feeder tree. There were no birds there, but she could hear the sleepy chirping of sparrows in the distance.

Standing beneath the tree in the softening snow, she wondered about family and the stories she'd been told. Riser, with his bravery and self-sacrifice, allowing Angel, Bandit, and Moonsie to survive. Chuck, mentored by Moonsie, protected by Angel, and guardian of the young humans. Bandit, a gentle maternal soul who expressed her affection for everyone, young and old, in her loving grooming. Moonsie, wise, patient, and calm. Fluffity, with her fearless and intrepid spirit. And Chairman, who for a large part of his life, had got it wrong.

Family was much more than just your littermates or your parents. Family could grow. Family could evolve. All anyone wanted, Misty suddenly realized, was to simply live their lives.

We all need food and shelter… and someone to love. Those cats who lived here before us, she thought affectionately, *were no ordinary cats. Their memories and their lessons are deep within us. And it will be up to Smokey and me to pass those lessons along to the kittens who will come to live with us. I hope we don't have long to wait.*

She padded back to the garage and snuggled down next to Smokey on the cushions. As they slept, the evening breeze shifted to the south, bringing the promise of spring and of new life.

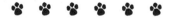

I lift the first kitten from the carrier. A tiny female with faint calico markings, she doesn't protest as I set her on my knee for a closer examination.

She has the most gorgeous eyes, and her whiskers are almost longer than she is. The second kitten, a larger male, makes a bit of a fuss when he is removed from the carrier. I smile at his spunk and set him down beside his sister. His fur is a sleek and shiny black, and he sports white whiskers and tiny white claws. The last kitten takes a little more convincing to get out of the carrier and seems to want to cuddle. I have no objection. His longer hair is tawny and silky with lovely dark dapples.

I watch with some trepidation as Misty and Smokey approach the newcomers. To my relief, Misty sniffs them from the tips of their tiny noses to the ends of their skinny little tails and gives them each a lick or two of approval.

Smokey seems a little more reserved and turns his back to collapse on the cushions. Resignedly, I wonder if his reaction will be a repeat of what happened when Chuck arrived. Instead, he rolls over and stretches, almost as if he's inviting the kittens to join him. To my delight, the kittens trot over and clumsily climb up on the cushions to rest on his soft stomach. And my eyes may be deceiving me, but did he actually just stretch out a front leg to gather them in a little closer?

Welcome, little ones. We've been waiting for you.

CHAPTER NINE

· ·

CALLIE, JET, AND LEO

"Settle down, youngsters," Smokey told them as they squirmed in closer to his warm stomach. "If you're living here, there are some rules to keep in mind."

The three newcomers looked up at him trustingly. "But first," Smokey continued with a smile, "I'm going to tell you a story about the cats who lived here before you. First, there was Riser…"

Printed in Canada